MESSAGE FOR THE TRIBE OF MANY COLORS

Message for the Tribe of Many Colors

Little Grandmother
(Kiesha Crowther)

Edited by Jennifer Ferraro

earth mother
PUBLISHING

Published by
Earth Mother Publishing
7 Avenida Vista Grande B7
Santa Fe, NM 87508
Web: www.earthmotherpublishing.com

To my personal angels living on Earth
who have inspired me to live by their
example, their egoless love and purity
of heart—the beautiful angels I proudly
know as my children and my brothers.

To my *anam cara,* who has held my hand
and supported me through the dark into
the light, and to my elder and grandfather,
Eesawu—your voice will always ring in
my ears. I honor and love you both.

Contents

Part III: Visions of the Present and the Future

Introduction

Inside these pages is a story that will move your heart and a message we hope will light a fire inside you—a passionate flame of love for Mother Earth. The purpose of this book is to reignite a deep remembrance within you of *who you really are*. You who are reading this are much greater than you can even imagine; indeed, you are a divine being who can change the future, who can change reality. You can become Love, and live from Love, and, by doing so, heal yourself, others, and Mother Earth. This is the essence of the message Little Grandmother has been guided to share now, as humanity stands at the threshold of an immense spiritual transformation that has been prophesied to come at this time on Earth by almost all ancient and indigenous cultures.

As we see all around us the imbalances and dangers in the way we have been living on Earth and sense that we are at an evolutionary turning point, the eyes of the world turn toward those messengers and wisdom keepers who are in direct contact with Spirit, with Earth herself, and with the sources of ancient wisdom. These sources speak of changes prophesied to come very soon to planet Earth, of what might be awaiting us. Although no one on the planet knows exactly what will happen, or when, some beings have been appointed special tasks, have been given information to share at this time. Little Grandmother is one of these beings, whom Spirit has asked to share a powerful and crucial message, a message for the "tribe of many colors"—for all us children of Mother Earth. We hope that this book will help open and awaken hearts and inspire many to follow the call of love for Mother Earth, the call of a vast beauty waiting for us when we *remember who we are*.

Little Grandmother is at the beginning of her journey, so this book will not present a biography or a completed picture of her work or message.

There is no doubt much more to come, and this book is intended be the first in a series of sharings. In it is a more detailed articulation of the message Little Grandmother has been sharing and teaching thus far as well as spiritual insights gleaned from her young life and experiences in nature, where she was taught by Mother Earth and Spirit. Although she is young and her path is still evolving and being revealed, we have heard the requests from people around the world wanting a fuller explanation of the message and a deeper glimpse into Little Grandmother's path. Though she has always stressed that it is the message, not the messenger, that matters, I think it is important for the reader to know something about Kiesha's journey to becoming Little Grandmother to fully understand and contextualize her message.

Growing up in a small, rural, Mormon farming community in Colorado, Kiesha had certain uncanny abilities and experiences that marked her as different, even at a young age. She could sense and communicate with animals and had encounters with voices that would speak to her, teaching specific lessons. She had no frame of reference for any of these things. Though her mother's side of the family primarily lives on a Native American reservation, Kiesha grew up with little exposure to these traditions. Raised a devout Mormon, there was no place for paranormal experiences: hearing voices, talking to spirits, or sensing things that others did not. In fact, she learned early on to never speak of such things and did not talk about these special abilities with anyone until she was twenty-eight years old and already a mother of two small children. She could not have foreseen how dramatically her life would soon change.

When Kiesha turned thirty, she was contacted by several indigenous elders who told her that the elders had been watching her since she was a child, that it was time for her to step into her role as shaman. They said they knew that the "grandmothers past" had been speaking to her and teaching her since she was a child. Kiesha was told that her role was to gather a "tribe of many colors." Her name, by which the ancestors and spirits recognized her, was "Little Grandmother."

At this point, Kiesha did not know what the word *shaman* meant. She had not read books on the subject and was not sure what the role entailed. Yet she was continually receiving guidance directly from spirits who would appear to her. She was told that she was one of twelve wisdom keepers on the planet at this pivotal time. Each of these wisdom keepers had been learning lessons from Mother Earth since he or she was a child. Each was receiving the same information and messages, though each had a different role to play. Kiesha was able to sense when things were happening to Mother Earth, when she was shifting, contracting, moving, being hurt, or being deeply effected in some way. Like the other wisdom keepers, Kiesha would be responsible for certain crystals that were to be placed back in the Earth, to strengthen Mother's Earth's ley lines and energy grid before the Great Shift was to happen. But most important, she would be responsible for sharing a message to help the children of Earth *remember who they are*. Kiesha's special purpose was to bring together people of every land, to gather together this tribe of every color for the purpose of changing the consciousness on planet Earth.

When all this happened so suddenly, Kiesha was awestruck. She struggled to take it all in and make sense of it. She had to pray very hard about what it all meant and what was being asked of her. Could she do it? Was it really her they were talking about? Had they made a mistake? She knew that her life would not be just her own anymore, that she would have to step out of anonymity and share her experiences, her childhood, her visions and visitations. She would be exposed and truly visible for the first time in her life. What if she failed? She would be stepping into the unknown, yet she would also finally be stepping into her soul's purpose. Deep inside, she had always known that she had come here for a very large purpose. After all those years of something feeling not right about her life as it was, everything finally fell into place: why she had suffered certain things as a child and learned to speak with Mother Earth, why she had received the teachings she had—it was to prepare her for this!

After several weeks of prayer and intense soul searching, Kiesha accepted her path to become shaman and her name "Little Grandmother." She was guided through the ceremony of initiation, which included fasting, prayer, and specific rituals. She was taught how to pray and to conduct specific healings and ceremonies. She had to absorb much very quickly, and in that first year, she became well aware of her lack of preparation and training. Why was she being asked to do this when she had clearly grown up away from indigenous ways and traditions, with no preparation other than what she had been taught directly from Spirit? She had to trust that there was a reason and that Spirit and the ancestors knew what they were doing. She prayed to do things correctly and to be open to guidance from Spirit on what was required of her, to help her with what she did not know.

In the months that followed, synchronistic and phenomenal things started to happen. Gifts, letters, and "medicine" began arriving in the mail from people all over the world, who recognized her and addressed her by her new name—"Little Grandmother." She received cards and letters as well as medicine shields, a sacred Earth drum, and ceremonial staves from individuals from across the Unites States, Canada, Australia, Africa, and South America. A couple living in Australia, from different indigenous tribes, had received a vision that they were to create medicine for the "white woman" called "Little Grandmother." With utmost care, prayer, and attention to spiritual guidance, they created her several shields designed with motifs and symbols specific to her, for her protection, as well as a sacred Earth drum that she was to use for prayer and for connecting to the ancestors.

As a child, Kiesha sought the wilderness as refuge and found a family among the creatures, trees, and plants. She arrived at a direct realization that few in modern civilization still have the opportunity to discover—that Mother Earth is a being and that Spirit is all around us in the living world, if only we listen and look. As a child, she was taught by what she refers to as "the other side," by voices and spirits who spoke to her. She was also taught through a kind of inner television screen that would appear to her, on which she would be shown certain images of places, people, events, and symbols. She felt very different growing up and often wondered if she was really a little crazy. I think many of us can relate to this sense of alienation around our spiritual experiences and knowings, especially when they are not confirmed by our religious upbringing or culture.

As this book shows, what she had to live through and learn in her spiritual journey to becoming Little Grandmother is in many ways a moving universal story about having faith in one's purpose and destiny. It speaks to the doubt, confusion, and pain that often accompany our journey to spiritual maturity, to becoming who we are meant to be. Ultimately, I think it shows that there is a greater purpose for things that happen to us than we imagine—and that those struggles we have faced and the wounds we have sustained can open us to guidance from Spirit and to greater beauty. This, to me, is a powerful dimension of her story and of the messages she has to share. It somehow grounds the other, more esoteric aspects of the message for many of us who do not receive direct messages from Spirit. This helps lift them from the realm of belief and faith.

Through knowing Kiesha, I have seen with my own eyes things that I otherwise may have doubted. I have been present when Kiesha has received information from Spirit and, at times, have even transcribed the messages coming through. Sometimes this information was so specific—about places of which she had never heard, places one could hardly make up by trying, such as Pumapunku. When she received esoteric information about the nature and purpose of this ancient place, which, to both of us, was a mystery, I doubted whether we would find it on any map. But there it was in Bolivia, with its H-shaped architecture, just as she had drawn in her notepad.

Sometimes she will receive a detailed vision of a mudslide or an earthquake happening in a particular country, and sure enough, when we search the news the next day, there has been a cataclysm in a particular place, as she had seen it. Sometimes spirits show up, plain as day to her. During a healing session, occasionally someone's deceased relative will suddenly show up in the room and pass on very detailed information meant for the person sitting there. She will describe the relative to a tee—what he or she is wearing and saying—while the living person sits there in tears, flabbergasted. This kind of thing I had only read about or seen on television before witnessing it firsthand. Interestingly, Kiesha cannot control when this happens or make it happen. It seems to happen when the spirit world decides that communication is necessary. Though I have always been a spiritual seeker and meditator, I had never experienced such phenomena before. These incidents have proven to me irrefutably the existence of the spirit world and the presence of dimensions of reality beyond what most of us perceive in our daily lives.

Kiesha and I met in 2006 at a women's spiritual retreat in Crestone, Colorado. Instantly, we became soul friends, and I have been privileged to be an intimate witness of her journey ever since. In hindsight, this retreat was what really started Kiesha on her path to becoming Little Grandmother. It was the first time she had stepped out of her small-town upbringing and done any kind of alternative spiritual retreat, especially among women. It was a huge opening. It was the first time she shared who she was publicly with others and felt safe enough to speak about some of her experiences.

The year we met, before she became Little Grandmother, she wrote out her life story to me in episodes, in long letters, sharing for the first time what she had experienced and learned from Spirit and Mother Nature since childhood. These letters often made me weep because of their poignancy. I grew increasingly convinced that Kiesha was no ordinary young woman—that she had some unique destiny. Her story, as she shared it with me through letter after letter, had a mythic dimension to it. Her healing process had begun, and she was unfolding like a flower that had long been closed up, burning up the pain and negativity that she had been holding on to for so long and that had nearly killed her. I sensed, even then, in those early days, that someday her story would be told—there were things in it that were important and that needed to be shared. I knew it would open hearts, as it had opened mine. But at that point, neither of us could have guessed what was in store for her, how her role would be much larger than we had imagined.

Though Kiesha has since been recognized as something special—as Little Grandmother—and has some unusual gifts and abilities, she is also quite human. She has had to dig down for the light, as have many others who have seen the darker aspects of humanity and who have known much pain and adversity. I feel that she is grounded in a basic humility that comes from losing, early on, certain things that others take for granted—and having to find a deeper reason to live. Yet, as any person notices as soon as he or she meets her, Kiesha has retained a striking innocence and purity of heart. I feel this is why she is able to fulfill the challenging responsibility of being shaman (one who walks between the worlds) and wisdom keeper. This purity of heart and *innocence* is key.

The challenges of the shamanic path are so daunting that it is amazing to me that so many people in the West *want* to be shamans. Hardly a week goes by that Kiesha does not face some severe physical pain, illness, challenge, or unusual phenomenon. These experiences can range from the merely unsettling to the downright debilitating. One must be very sensitive—and yet this sensitivity makes one physically and psychically open to that much more pain, negativity, and the entire spectrum of human emotion and experience. Becoming well known has not always been easy for such a sensitive being!

Interestingly, Kiesha has never sought fame or recognition, yet within three years' time, her message has reached millions of people all over the world. This could not have been accomplished by an unworldly, uneducated country girl without the help of Spirit. As one who has witnessed this, it seemed clear that something big was in the works; otherwise, there was no explanation for so many coming to know of this young woman named "Little Grandmother" and wanting to hear her.

Little Grandmother really only started to become known in 2009, after videographer Bob Keeton videotaped her speaking to a crowd of fifty people in Santa Fe. She was describing for those who had not been present the powerful three-day ceremony she had led that April. This had been Little Grandmother's first public ceremony. She had been asked to lead it by those coordinating the official Return of the Ancestors international gathering of indigenous elders on Hopi land in Arizona, an event planned in conjunction with Hopi and Mayan prophecies. She had been terrified beforehand, having never led a public ceremony before. She truly had to step into a greater power to do it, utterly trusting Spirit to guide her. Most of the people present at that ceremony said afterward that it was the single most powerful spiritual gathering in which they had ever taken part. (You can read about this ceremony in detail in the chapter "Return of the Ancestors.") We all felt we had taken part in something truly pivotal and of global spiritual significance. As many sensed, and as Little Grandmother actually saw and confirmed, the ancestors were in attendance—thousands of them—and even participated with us in this ceremony.

While the ceremony itself had been powerful for all those who had taken part, so was Kiesha's recounting of it at this talk, which happened about a month later. She managed to capture the energy and sacred emotion that had been present during the ceremony and transmit it to those listening. She had a special ability to open people's hearts. Bob felt that the talk had a really important message and spiritual transmission to share and asked if he could post the video on YouTube. Kiesha agreed. Within six months, the video of this talk had gone viral and had been seen by thousands of people. Kiesha was being contacted by hundreds of people from all over the world who were moved, who felt passionately about healing the Earth and ourselves and about learning to live from the heart, in harmony with nature. Invitations to travel, speak, and conduct sacred ceremonies began pouring in from all over the globe.

Since then, in a very short amount of time, hundreds of thousands have been drawn to Little Grandmother's heartfelt message and presence. They are inspired to come together in unity for the sake of our beautiful, precious Mother Earth, to try to shift the prevailing consciousness on the planet from ego and mind back to Love, just as the indigenous elders and wise ones on the planet have been teaching us. A great wave is gathering. It is a coming together of the children of Mother Earth as one tribe, as one heart united, to change the way we live and experience life on this planet. Toward this end, Little Grandmother has been traveling and speaking, to share the messages she is given by Spirit and Mother Earth. And yet another powerful aspect of her sacred work remains the specific ceremonies for Mother Earth (some public and some not) she is guided to do, which help strengthen and awaken Mother Earth's energy grid system and bring forth the forgotten wisdom we will need to save ourselves and the planet in this pivotal time of transformation. It is our heartfelt hope that this book will serve this cosmic purpose as well.

Little Grandmother has been asked to gather together a tribe of many colors. So who is this tribe of many colors? It is all Earth's children, every color, nation, and creed, united as one heart. It is those who are ready to come together in their hearts and affirm the unity of existence within the diversity of life, to care for each other and work together to create a more beautiful world. It is those who are ready for a new way of being; a new Earth; a more beautiful, sane, caring, balanced, and evolved existence.

We want to save Mother Earth and to evolve with her into something extraordinary. We do not want to abandon her or to hurt, abuse, and neglect her anymore. We want to see her on her throne, abundant and healthy, as we worship each precious blade of grass, each drop of water, and know the intense beauty and sacredness of this existence we are given to experience. More and more of us are on fire with love for this creation and believe in Love as the way in which we will be guided home to who we really are—magnificent beings able to create our reality. We want to create a more caring, loving, reverent way of being with each other and our Mother. We are one heart, one family—the children of Mother Earth. As Little Grandmother often says, "We are the strongest of the strong," the ones who came to Earth at this time of challenge and high stakes to change the world. We are the ones prophesied to be here at this time on Earth; we are "the ones we have been waiting for," as the Hopi prophecy says. We are the Tribe of Many Colors, the ones who will change the world. We are ready to listen and to learn.

A Note about the Structure of this Book

Part I, "Lessons in the Wilderness," gives a very human framework to some of the more esoteric spiritual information discussed later in the book and describes some important episodes and spiritual lessons in Kiesha's childhood and early life. The "wilderness" here is both literal and symbolic—referring not only to Nature but to those areas of life that are difficult and of which we struggle to make meaning. Part II, "Remember Who You Are," focuses on the inner aspects of the message that Little Grandmother has been guided to share—those things that human beings need to remember and to which they must become attuned to shift into a higher consciousness. Part III, "Visions of the Present and the Future," shares information and teachings of an esoteric and prophetic nature that Little Grandmother has received directly from her sources of guidance. She shares these things from her own heart and wants to make it very clear that she does not represent any indigenous people, tribe, group, or individual in doing so. She does not attempt to present indigenous or Native American teachings or traditions but only that which she has been directly taught by Spirit and guided to share.

—Jennifer Ferraro

PART I
Lessons in the Wilderness

Beginning the Journey:
The Heart as Foundation and Way

Beloved reader,

My purpose in writing this book is to help humanity connect to the heart—the heart being the very foundation of all knowledge, all inspiration and divine understanding. When I have traveled and spoken to people all around the world, many have asked me if I would write a book about the things I speak of. With all my love and gratitude, and after much hard work (I thought public speaking was hard!), I give this book to you, my dear brother or sister. This book is written for you, to help you realize just how divine, majestic, and powerful you are. You, reader, are the answer to your own prayers. You are a spark of Creator, and you can change the world simply by living in love, by remembering that it was your own higher self—your Great I AM—that chose to come to this planet at this exact moment, for a very special purpose.

There are many great books and authors out there who describe theories and speculations about the changes that are happening and about to happen on the planet. It is easy to get worried about what others are writing and saying about the future, so I would offer this simple advice: whatever does not lead to your greater peace, inspiration, and sense of loving gratitude for this life, set aside. You don't need it!

What you need to know is already inside you, within your own heart. What works on the level of mind only can only heal the mind—it cannot help us enter our hearts. It is the awakening of the heart and the realization of *who we really are* that will change the way we live, that will change our very future. And this is exactly what we are being asked to do now by many indigenous elders and wisdom keepers on the planet as well as by the many light beings who are here watching and helping us. We are asked to start living from our hearts and to remember how divine, amazing, and vast we actually are. Sounds simple, right? It's not as hard as our minds would have us think.

We are human hearts, beating with living emotion and feeling. We connect and love each other not through our shared ideas of things but through shared feeling. And so, in these pages, I share with you, dear brother or sister, not only the information and teachings I have been receiving from my spirit guides and teachers but also some of my personal journey. I hope that these personal stories will open your heart. Without this, I might not seem real to you, and the message I have to share with you might seem too otherworldly or strange. I am a simple person, and therefore this book is written as simply as possible, from my heart to yours, sharing what I know to be true based on my guidance from Spirit. The most important thing is to connect on a heart level because this is where we come together and can see one another as another "myself." We are of one heart and can understand and therefore love each other more deeply than we realize.

We are truly gods and goddesses. We are all spiritual equals, and no one's journey is any greater than another's to Great Spirit. Whether you are a stay-at-home parent, a carpenter, an author, a businessperson, or a sales clerk, you have it within you to change this world. You have all the wisdom and divine Love of the Creator within your spirit, and it is time to step into your true being. It is time to remember what we know and have forgotten—that we are Love, that this creation is the very essence of Love. Knowing this, we can and will change our world.

I promise you that what I share in this book has been my experience—whether you believe in or are on board with such things as star beings, spirit guides, and Earth-change prophesies is not so important. Trust your heart to know what is real for you, and use whatever you can from these words. What matters most is that you remember your heart and know that Love truly is the answer to every question. Your heart will lead you to a cosmic dimension of being that we cannot even imagine now but soon will all know.

Being in your heart will connect you to the heart of Mother Earth, and she will protect you, feeling your vibration of love and gratitude. We are choosing what will happen to us in the near future by every thought, feeling, and breath we have. Right now, we are in a brief window of time when it is urgent to understand this and to start remembering. I have been shown that immense changes are about to happen on planet Earth, and after them, humanity will never be the same again. We are about to embark on a spiritual adventure that no one in the universe has witnessed before, an evolutionary leap that is unprecedented in the whole cosmos. While evolution has always happened, it has never happened as rapidly as it is happening now for the children of planet Earth. How exactly this will play out no one is certain, but many of us are being shown things and are being given information to assist in the process, and this is what I share with you in this book.

In these pages, I describe the experiences I have had with star beings, light beings, my spirit guides and ancestors, and Mother Earth herself—and what they have been teaching me. I share what I believe is possible on this planet as far as the expansion of consciousness and the changes and shifts on Earth that are occurring already and are most likely to occur, but most important, I share with you how you can assist in this shift of consciousness and prepare yourself to ascend with Mother Earth to a higher way of being. I hope this book will move your heart and inspire you to awaken to the mystery and beauty of the opportunity before us.

What an amazing time to be alive on planet Earth. All our souls have chosen to be born on Earth at this time. We chose to come here and to witness and experience this cosmic event—which the whole universe is watching—to experience it firsthand. We are the "strongest of the strong" souls who have ever been on planet Earth—and there is nothing to fear, if we stay in our hearts and attune ourselves to Love. Our love vibration can attune us to higher dimensions of reality that exist alongside our three-dimensional reality, and from here come guidance, knowledge, and wisdom, which will hasten the evolution of human beings. Mother Earth is in the process of cleansing herself of negativity and the toxins that are killing her so that she can be reborn. If we remember this, we will not see only devastation around us but the light and love that is guiding us toward something more beautiful than we can imagine. We know how to do this, and we will do it together. We will remember where we come from and what we once knew—and then we will go beyond even that.

Let us gather our hearts together and grow the Love vibration on this planet. Let us gather as one tribe, the children of Mother Earth, and unite as a single heart in love with our beloved Mother and this precious creation. Let us promise each other never to give up on this Earth, never to give in to fear and despair—never to give up on each other. Love is the most profound, abundant, and least understood energy on Earth, and it is through Love that we will create a paradise like we have never before seen on Earth. We will shift into a higher dimension of being and become the divine beings we were always meant to become.

I am so thankful to be here on this beautiful planet with you, on this amazing journey together. May we remember who we are and that we are one heart, always. May we create a new Earth and a new humanity together and know that after every death, there is rebirth; after the storm comes a rainbow. May we see it, and feel it in our hearts, and not be afraid to step forward, hand in hand, into the greatness that is awaiting us.

In love and gratitude,

Little Grandmother

Speaking with the Animals

From as far back as I can remember, the animals have been my dearest of friends, friends with whom I have had very real conversations. Since I was a child, I have been able to talk to and sense animals in a very special way. This was never overtly discussed in my family but was just something that simply was. It was natural for all of us and was known by others in the small community in which I grew up. My father was a farmer and a ranch hand; therefore I was very lucky as a child to grow up in the wilderness and in very close proximity to farm animals, not to mention to all the wildlife that abounds in the mountains of Colorado.

I remember one moment in particular. While I was young, I first realized I could sense life energy in an animal. It left an impression on me I shall never forget. The days were growing shorter by that time of year; it must have been early February by the amount of snow still on the ground outside the little farmhouse in which we were living. My sister Kelsy and I stood in the kitchen, our handmade pajamas dangling just past our knees and our bare feet pressed to the cold linoleum floor. We couldn't have been more than four and five at the most, as we watched for our father to come in the door at any moment with the calves. Mom was heating up the oven and moving about quickly, getting this and that ready for when Pa brought in the little ones. I couldn't quite grasp what was happening, but we knew there was a rush and a panic in the air as Mom started to boil the water. Kelsy and I stood hand in hand, our eyes fixed on the back door, when Pa flung it open and the freezing night air hit our skin. There stood my father with two large calves over each shoulder as he pushed his way into the house. It started to become very clear what all the fuss was about when I saw that the little calves were not moving. They were half frozen to death.

Mom lowered the oven door so that it lay open, and Pa carefully placed the calves one by one on the door to be warmed. I watched closely as the ice on one of the calves' noses started to melt; my tears started to swell. I just couldn't bear watching the calves die. I tucked my pajamas under my knees as I knelt down and placed my little hand on the little calf's head, and there in that farmhouse, buried in a snowstorm, I knew for the first time what life energy felt like. I remember it clear as day, this warm tingle, not much different from the feeling of one's hand coming back to life after having fallen asleep, but with a buzzing about it as well. At first I thought the little calf was warming up so I must be feeling the heat coming back into its body, but there was something more. I could feel life coming back inside the body of the animal. I could feel it, taste it, hear it—the little calf was going to be okay. I knew it before the little thing ever made a sound or flinched the slightest bit. I jumped up at that moment, and Kelsy and I went straight to making the calves bottles of warm milk. My parents had their doubts, but soon the calves were both up and standing under the weight of their own little bodies, sucking down the milk as fast as they could.

Some might think it strange for a child to be able to feel life energy or experience so many senses at once, with taste, sound, texture and sometimes even a number being part of the experience. Maybe it is not strange at all, given that my mother went into labor with me in our barn among birthing cows and calves. It had been a huge snowstorm, and my mother, who was nine months pregnant, had been trying to help my father pull a calf from a new, inexperienced heifer. She ended up slipping and falling and went into labor. So perhaps it was due to this—even as a toddler, I loved to go out and be with the calves and lambs in the barn.

I knew what an animal was feeling and what it needed; I knew it through taste, texture, color, and emotion. I could tune in to an animal's feelings and soothe them, speaking to the animal without words. I could also sense when animals were near without seeing them. This did not come without some hard-earned lessons, of course; one of the first times I can remember feeling the cry of an animal for help was years ago. The whole family was lying around the living room watching TV when, out of nowhere, I got this feeling of complete panic inside my chest, the fear that the lambs were being attacked by wild dogs. I sat there thinking about it for a moment and listening to see if I could hear any ruckus out back. I talked myself out of what I was feeling and went on watching the program on TV. Then I heard a voice, a big voice say, "Go!" I jumped up and looked around at my family, but it was apparent that none of them had heard the command.

Finally, I decided to wander outside and take a look at the lambs just to put my mind at ease. What I saw when I opened that back door horrified me. My stomach sank and my legs almost buckled as I saw our favorite little lamb, Abby, hanging from a dog's mouth, her white fleece covered in blood. I yelled for my father and I ran to help Abby. When the dog had dropped the lamb and scattered, Abby lay there with puncture wounds in her throat and all along her little body. I sat with her for days, even weeks, taking turns with my brothers and sisters feeding her and nursing her back to health, and I made a promise that from that day forward, if I was ever to hear an animal speak again, I would listen!

People who know me well get a kick out of how I can sense specific animals from far away, before I see them. While driving on the highway, I can sense that elk will be on the road within the next mile or that hidden in the brush is a bear or rabbit or raccoon. Each animal has a different taste and texture to me and a feeling that comes when it is near. Although this is hard to describe, it is really a mixing together of various sensations and feelings. For example, if there is an owl, I will taste bitter dark chocolate. I will sense the deep, dark color of purple and the feel of crushed velvet. All these things mixed together tell me about the animal, its sex, how far away it is, and if I focus in closely, what it is feeling and communicating. An elk, by contrast, tastes like bark or dried grass in my mouth. Science may try to pinpoint how this all works—I am not sure myself how it works, but only that this mixture of simultaneous sensations all of a sudden tells me what and where the animals are.

If it is nighttime, I always put on my "critter-dar," as I jokingly call it. If someone else is driving, all of a sudden I will tell him or her to slow down because I know that there are going to be two elk in the road within two bends. It's a quirk of mine that has come in very handy many times, especially driving between Santa Fe and Colorado by the

San Antonio Mountain, where elk are almost always out on the road at night, causing accidents.

I mentioned earlier that my special ways with animals were never really discussed when I was growing up. My family and others in the town knew this oddity about me and would ask for my assistance with their animals when it was needed, but it was never questioned or addressed or given much importance—and it embarrassed me, too. Raised in a small, conservative, Mormon community, this was certainly not something I was going to talk about! I always felt very different and knew that I didn't fit in with my peers. I was already known as the tomboy who would rather run off and talk to animals than to people. The Mormon religion is not tolerant of anything outside its own beliefs, to say the least, so I knew never to speak of my experiences with nature or, later, with spirits and the voices that were communicating with me. I learned to keep much of what I experienced inside—afraid that I was some sort of freak or crazy person—and it was not until I was in my late twenties that I actually spoke of these things to another human being for the first time.

Animals as Loving Family

When I would run off to my special place not far from the town where two rivers meet and the water springs warm from the Earth, sheltered by huge cottonwood trees, I was most often alone. But I was also safe because human beings could not find me there. I would sit within this beautiful cove of cottonwood trees, in this valley surrounded by distant mountains, and feel sheltered, protected, where the trees, plants, and animals truly became my family.

In the winter in Colorado, at eighty-five hundred feet altitude, it becomes very, very cold. I seldom had more than a jacket, a backpack, an old tin coffee can in which I boiled water, and whatever food I could stuff into my sack on the way out the door—usually a potato or two, an orange, a can of beans. I remember making a fire in my fire pit, and afterward, using an old camping trick my father taught me, I would gather the rocks used to make the campfire ring and put them inside my clothes, then sleep on the Earth where the fire had been so as not to freeze to death. Sometimes, when it wasn't too cold, I would cover myself with soil and leaves, burying myself in the Earth as if it were a blanket—and it was.

But the elk helped me, too. There was a resident herd of elk in this special place, maybe eighteen or nineteen of them. When I would go down to my little cove, right across the river, I could see the herd, which would bed down at night in the long, soft grasses there. If I would move slowly, at their pace, they would let me come to them and sleep among them, with their young ones. Animals speak not only through their emotions but through their body language. I would closely observe their ears—were they pricked upright or relaxed? Did the mothers stamp the ground or move lazily? If a mother barked at me, I would back up and sit down. But most important was the expression in the eyes of the animals. I would watch the mothers' eyes closely, keeping watch for the alertness and glassy shock of fear that would slowly turn into a calm, relaxed, sleepy look. I would wait for this change before I would attempt to move into the circle. The elk always put the young in the center, and the adults' body heat kept them warm and alive. They let me lie with their young in the center and kept me very much alive. To this day, these elk and their young, who are now adults, are my family. Since I have been an adult, I have returned to this spot to check on them and visit them several times. Most of them shy away from me a great deal now, but every now and then, one of the older females will let me come up next to them with that old, familiar, subtle language we had so long ago.

Animal Spirits and Totems

All the creatures of the Earth carry a medicine and are constantly offering us humans spiritual help, guidance, and love, though we seldom even see it or recognize it. I often wear an owl talon around my neck, especially when I am doing ceremony or speaking in public. This is no ordinary memento or talisman—this is powerful medicine given to me from a very great friend of mine, one who changed my life. The owls have always been a huge part of my life, especially great horned owls. A family of great horned owls lived in the trees across the road from my childhood home the whole time I was growing up. My great grandmother was the first one to introduce them to me as we would often go near the huge pines to pick the wild asparagus. We stood there hand in hand, looking up into the pine tree, where was perched the most beautiful great horned owl I had ever seen. His eyes seemed to pierce my very soul; we just looked at one another, not saying a word, not moving an inch—just looking with great fascination.

This owl lived right outside my door in the big pine tree, where he had been raised from an owlet and now he had grown to have his own mate and nest. This owl and his mate would come every year and hatch beautiful baby owls. Every time I would venture out into the wilderness, I would peer up into the sky, and without fail, there he would be, flying overhead with me. There he would stay with me, perched nearby in the trees. This owl would even bring me food. He would bring me rodents, and once, he brought me a piece of fish. When he brought me mice, I would try to do my best to pretend to be eating what he had brought me, with exaggerated chewing and "yummy" sounds, then offer him some. I couldn't bear to hurt my friend's feelings after he had been so loving. But I just couldn't bring myself to eat the mice, no matter how grateful I was for the gift!

The owl is one of my protector animals—and I will always be grateful for the care and tenderness they have offered. But this one special friend of mine was soon to depart the Earth, and before he left, he gave me a gift I will always treasure.

Around age fourteen, I was lazily walking into my grandfather's old barnyard when, all of a sudden, I heard a "swooshing" sound and turned around. The great horned owl hit me in the chest full on, and as I recovered from the blow and grasped onto him, I tried to pull him away from me out of sheer reflex, but the owl's talon had lodged in my chest. I held the owl close to me, feeling his weak heart beat with his talon still there, lodged in me, as the owl breathed his last few breaths. To this day, I have a scar above my heart where the talon lodged, and I have worn that talon around my neck ever since. My friend chose to spend his last moments with me, and he marked my flesh and my being. That owl is still my best friend, and owls remain a constant presence in my life—when I am truly in need, they appear and make their presence felt. At those times, I go outside and call to them and wait for that tender sound out of the invisible night, the sound of home and family to me.

I am not special in that I can communicate with and sense animals. Everyone can speak with animals—we've just been taught not to, that we can't, and that paying too much attention to animals is silly. We've been taught that what we think means more than what we feel. This is the main obstacle between us and being able to communicate and work with animals. Animals have a spirit, just as Mother Earth herself has a spirit. Mother Earth will talk to you, help you, and teach you, just as the animals will, if only we tune in and learn to listen. Animals communicate through feelings, not through words.

When an animal is scared, you can feel that it is scared or panicked. You can feel its need to choose between fight or flight. You can feel its fears, sadness, or emotional reactions. We just need to open our capacity to feel and sense—not to think about everything and depend so much on what we see with our eyes and figure out with our minds. It is much like a mother with a young child. Before that child can speak and physically express what he or she is feeling or needing, a mother knows. You know without a doubt when your child is afraid, hurt, scared, or sick because you can feel it. How many mothers have had the experience of waking up a moment before their babies wake up or knowing without a doubt when something is wrong? There is no explaining with a rational mind how we do this, but it is real. We can feel and know these things. I believe it is safe to say that our feelings about something can be truer than our thoughts about something. What we feel in our heart, in our gut, is our connection to our higher selves, more than what we think about something. So is it really far-fetched to say that anyone who is attuned to the animal world can *feel* what the animals are saying? The great part about this is that we *all* can; we just have to train ourselves into that way of feeling.

For example, I cannot rationally explain how it is that I see a particular animal in the center of each person's chest. I never read books on shamanism or Native American spirituality and so was unaware of the craze over animal totems and all that has been written about how to find them and work with them. It was something of which I never spoke, especially in my early years of Mormon training, but I could always see a particular animal that is with each person. Most people have one animal with them whose spirit has chosen to guide them and be with them through life—but I have encountered some people with two. I cannot explain this rationally, but clear as day, I can see a particular and often quite specific animal in the center of each person's chest.

When I tell the person what animal I see with him or her, most often, this knowledge comes as no surprise. Either the person had sensed it already, the person has had a long-standing relationship with that animal, or he or she had been told by some other shaman or medicine person the same thing. Sometimes, though, it is unexpected, and some people are even disheartened when they find out what animal I perceive to be with them. One needs to understand that no animal is greater or lesser than another in its being and in the medicine, lessons, and protection it offers. Whereas everyone wants to have the mountain lion, bear, wolf, or some other so-called powerful animal as a totem, few understand the power of badger medicine or the beautiful gifts of the skunk, or even the mouse, as spirit protector.

Many people have had encounters with the animal that is their spirit helper—and not necessarily pleasant encounters. I know one woman who was bitten by a mouse the day before I told her that her animal totem was the mouse. If you have had an important run-in or encounter with a particular animal, say, being bitten, it just may be that this animal has much to teach you and offer you and is trying to get you to pay attention to it. That animal may be a spirit protector for you. In the realm of the sacred, the greatest gifts often accompany something painful or seemingly adversarial. I have learned this myself, having been bitten by a rattlesnake and kicked by a horse, along with many other deep experiences with animals, both pleasant and unpleasant, many of which changed my life.

Messages from the Animals

As I've said before, sometimes our overthinking leads us to doubt what our bodies and feelings are telling us from the animal world. Yet animals carry much wisdom for us and are constantly interacting with us on subtle levels, when we tune in to their vibration and energy.

I'd like to share something that recently happened to me. I was giving a workshop outside Phoenix, Arizona, and was inwardly preparing myself for the day. As I stepped outside into the garden to pray, I could feel the presence of an animal nearby, so I stilled myself and tuned in. I was trying to get a read from my senses to tell me what animal was near. I could sense the texture of tall, dead grass running through my fingers and the smell of wet, dark soil as well as the number 4. Suddenly, a bobcat appeared directly in front of me, a few feet away, perched on top of the adobe wall of the garden. It immediately engaged me in a conversation. Others who were milling around nearby saw this and stopped to watch the encounter with wide eyes.

As some of you may know, bobcats are extremely elusive and rarely come near humans, especially in broad daylight. The bobcat and I stood a few feet apart for several long moments, just looking at each other. We exchanged love for one another, and then she began to tell me that she had come to give me a message. She told me that I had been undergoing a process of purification and that now things would be unblocked for me. She told me things about this desert land on which we stood—that it would become more lush in the future and that sacred ceremony had been done there in times past by the native people of the area. And most important, she told me that I needed to listen more to the animals and creatures because they are constantly trying to communicate teachings and messages to me. After she communicated this, she shifted her energy to listening for a quiet moment. Then, with a single exchange of love and blessing, she said she had to get back to her kittens and gently leaped away and disappeared. I could feel her presence in the area for the duration of the workshop.

Some of you may have experienced such direct communications from animals. Just as when I receive messages from Spirit or from a particular spirit guide, the message comes not in spoken words but in a direct transmission of understanding that is somehow a blending of all senses, feelings, intuitions, vibrations, colors, and tastes. If I were to try to figure this out, or logically explain it, I would entirely miss the message that was being transmitted.

One of the greatest challenges people of our highly rational, high-tech age face is how to trust our feelings, intuitions, and imaginations again.

These are our direct links to the rest of the creatures and life-forms on the planet. If we want to be in the right relationship to Mother Earth, we must allow ourselves to feel again, opening our senses and hearts to what we cannot see or explain. If we can do this, the animals will help us as they have always been willing to, and we will regain a richness of extended family and a sense of belonging that we had long ago lost.

All Things Are Alive with Energy

Spirit has shown me time after time how all things are alive with energy. Our physical world is living and pulsing, yet the majority of us have forgotten this, simply because we cannot see it with our eyes. We often see only the surface of things, the seeming solidity of matter. Yet it is this energy that is keeping us alive and nothing else. Science can even measure this energy now. We are one living, breathing, pulsing organism. We are alive because of the energy that Mother Earth gives us from the soles of our feet, keeping us connected to the web of life, giving us our breath. This energy is there for us every moment that we are in bodies, to sustain and nourish us, to replenish us. Yet we do not use it as we were meant to. We have forgotten how to use Earth energy and connect into the life source.

I remember how, as a teenager, I was awakened to seeing energy and color in things. I grew up in an area of southern Colorado renowned for its mysterious phenomena, sightings of strange lights, and UFOs: the San Luis Valley. This valley is also held sacred by many Native American tribes because it falls within the sacred triangle of Ute Mountain, Mount Blanca, and San Antonio Mountain in what is known as the bloodless valley. I have seen some strange things growing up there, as many other residents have. I have had a huge red light hover over my home on several occasions and have had several encounters with beings from other dimensions. I am not sure if the following incident would qualify as extraterrestrial, but it forever changed my life and how I perceive things.

Encounter with a Being of Light

One magical night, I was camping under the stars at my special place by the river. It had just grown dark, and I was lying there looking at the stars and listening to the wind in the trees. Then I saw what I thought looked like tractor lights in the field behind the trees. I could see the lights coming in and out, and I thought someone must be plowing, unusual as it was to be plowing at night. But these lights were blue, and I thought how odd that a tractor would have blue lights—I had never seen that before. As I watched the lights come closer and closer, a strange feeling came over me. It was a warmth, almost like warm water being poured from the tip of my head all down to my feet. It was the most soothing, calm, beautiful feeling. As the light came closer, right up to me, I could see that it was no longer just a blue light but a woman. Her hair was long and wavy, pulled back at the edges of her face in a long braid at the back of her head, where it hung down over her flowing gown. In the moment, I remember thinking that she looked something like what I would imagine Guinevere or a medieval princess to look like. Her long dress was finely embroidered at the wrists and hem, yet she was transparent and shimmering, entirely made of blue light and, at the same time, of music.

She came toward me and placed her hand on my face, her palm against my cheek. It was unlike anything I'd ever felt before. There was no pressure where her hand rested on my face, only warmth. She did not speak in words but in sound, in vibration. It was like music, but unlike any music I had ever heard—it was heavenly, celestial. In some indescribable way, she *was* music. The last thing I recall before I fell asleep was the warmth of her palm on my face and the sound of this music unlike any instrument I had ever heard.

When I woke up the next morning, everything was different. I tried to make sense of the encounter. It seemed almost like a dream, but I knew I had been awake. Something had happened to me. The lady was gone, yet I was left with something quite extraordinary. My eyes were different somehow; my way of seeing and perceiving had been changed. I could see new color in everything. I could perceive colors and the movement of energy in every blade of grass, in the trees, in the animals. I used to call it "seeing dots" because I could see colors in clusters, almost like pixilated dots, within everything. I am not sure exactly how this relates to seeing auras, but I think it is different because I see these colors within the body of the living thing itself. I think of it as seeing life energy. Some trees have more light and more color-vibration-energy in them than others, just as some humans have more light than others and have more color in certain places in their bodies than in other places at any given time.

It is tempting to want to separate light-color-vibration-energy, but in reality, these are all the same thing but appear differently through the filter of our human sense faculties. A color has a certain vibration, sound, texture, taste, and so on, and these all work together to tell me information about a living thing. This is how I am able to sense an animal nearby before seeing it. I get a certain taste in my mouth and feel a certain texture that comes with it. Each animal is different. I believe that soon we will all be able to perceive this and to work with vibration and energy in ways we have long forgotten as human beings. We all have this capacity but have gotten out of rhythm with Mother Earth and have forgotten how to perceive things spiritually, with a deeper vision.

Giving and Receiving Earth Energy

One thing I have been taught by Spirit and asked to share is that it's extremely important for us to start using our energy correctly again. We need to learn how to give and receive energy from Mother Nature rather than continually trying to get our energy from other human beings. Somewhere along the line, we became disassociated from nature and came to rely too much on other human beings for our basic sustenance and sense of well-being. There is an energetic give-and-take within every human interaction, and this has become the basis of our sense of self—how we are perceived and energetically received by others. For example, in any conversation, there is usually one person who gives energy and one who takes it—sometimes it is fairly balanced, but more often, it is not. On the basis of this energetic relationship that happens without us even being aware of it, we either feel good about ourselves and energized or slightly depleted and minimized by our interactions with other human beings. Unconsciously, we are often looking for energy from others to feed ourselves, to feel good, worthy, and vital. This was not supposed to be our primary way of charging ourselves, of making ourselves feel good.

We humans must learn to give and receive energy from the plants, the trees, the rivers, the oceans, and the Earth herself. When we fill ourselves with Mother Earth energy, we do not need to take energy from each other or from any other limited source. Mother Earth's energy, which is really Love energy, is limitless, abundant, and ever present. As long as we are here, in these bodies, this life energy is within us and all around us, offering itself. And unlike other resources of Earth that human beings have exploited and not replenished, this energy cannot be depleted. The more we connect with it and use it, the more life energy we create, and the more we have to give back to Mother Earth in the form of love, gratitude, and joy.

You can literally go outside and breathe in the energy from a tree until you are filled up, balanced, and connected again to source. Any living thing has boundless energy to sustain and nourish you—an acorn, a leaf, an apple, a stone, a mountain. If you feel weak, depressed, needy, or sick, go outside and breathe in the living energy of the natural world, feeling how you are it and it is you. You do not need to think anything in particular. What you believe about yourself doesn't matter, and what others believe of you doesn't matter. If you pay attention to what is alive around you, then your thoughts about who you are and what you think don't matter so much.

Why do you feel so good after you have been walking outdoors in the woods or sitting by a stream? Because you have just charged yourself—it's as if you are a battery and you have just been plugged in and recharged. With so many people now having no daily contact with Mother Nature and not taking the time to connect to living things in this way, we are missing out on a huge source of balance and sustenance. We are getting sicker and more imbalanced because our energies are constantly scattered and depleted by our lifestyles, without getting replenished regularly by Mother Nature. Everything you need to feel good is all around you, in the living, breathing natural world.

If we, as individuals, can do this each day—take the time to connect to and breathe in the living energy of Earth—it will drastically affect our lives and our world. We do not feel the need to be heard, to be in charge, because we do not need to gather our energy from other human beings to feel good. It doesn't matter what you do for a living if you do not need to get your sense of worth and well-being from such a thing. When you are connected to Nature and charged with life force, you no longer care how you are perceived by others because human beings are not all that exists. The living, breathing beings of the universe also perceive you, communicate with you, and know you. The natural world becomes more real than the society that structures our lives and tells us who we are and what we're worth. Whether you make millions as a famous author or you're a stay-at-home mom, you are not higher or lower. Filling ourselves with living Earth energy, we do not need to be addicted to other people, their love, or their perception of us. This liberates a huge amount of energy for us, for joy and creation. All the energy we need to support us is there waiting for us. We just need to breathe it in, connect with it, let it heal and help us.

There is plenty for all human beings to be constantly filled. Unlike our usual scarcity thinking, this natural abundance of living energy creates more abundance and is never scarce. This life energy is our greatest gift, and it is time we start using it again. We are here as creators. We are gods and goddesses, here to create beauty and to love. In love, everything is possible. And in connecting with the life energy of Mother Earth, our source, we connect to the immense fount of Love that surrounds us. This Love is actually the very substance of Mother Earth and the purpose of life.

Practice: Breathing in Earth Energy

This is a very simple yet very powerful practice I was taught by Spirit and specifically asked to share with others. When you are feeling out of balance or when you want to ground yourself and connect to Mother Earth, do this breathing exercise. I often have people do this before I do a healing session with them because it gets their energy flowing correctly and helps move blockages in particular chakras, places where the flow of life energy has become stuck or congested. It will also help open you to spiritual guidance and prepare you for deeper states of prayer and meditation. It is a powerful way to release what is blocking you and to connect to the source of all life.

Stand with your bare feet on the Earth. You can do this indoors as well, but take your shoes off. Start by breathing the color green, the color of Earth energy, up through the soles of your feet; feel this Earth energy filling your cells and nourishing every inch of you. With the first inhalation, bring it up as far as your knees, then exhale it down and out through the soles of your feet, back into the Earth.

On the second inhalation, bring this green energy up to the base of your pelvis (first chakra), and exhale it back into the Earth, feeling it enshroud your thighs, your knees, and your ankles and move back down through your feet. As you are doing this, if you have trouble connecting to any particular area of your body and feeling the energy fill you, continue with the breaths up to that area until you feel ready to move on.

On the third inhalation, bring the energy up to your lower pelvis, just below the navel (second chakra), and release it back downward into the Earth. Be sure to focus on each particular part of your body as you descend the energy; do not just skim over but visualize and feel the energy traveling down and filling your limbs, your muscles, and your blood, bones, and cells.

On the fourth inhalation, bring the energy up to your mid-belly (third chakra) and feel it circulating and penetrating your solar plexus. Many of us carry a lot of repressed emotion in this area of our bodies, which is tied to our will and sense of empower-ment, the overall feeling of who we are. You may need to breathe several times to this area. Let the healing Earth energy gently open your belly and loosen those places that are tight, that are holding on to old energies and fears. When you feel relaxed and open and you can feel a warmth spreading here, then you know you can move on.

On the fifth inhalation, breathe the energy up to your chest (fourth chakra) and feel it envelope and penetrate your heart. Feel it expand in your chest cavity, your lungs, and your ribs. The heart area carries so much old emotion, and many of us have deep hurts here. Gently let Mother Earth touch this place in you. Do this breath as many times as necessary, until you feel warmth spreading, until you feel a relaxing and an opening of this area.

Let whatever you have been holding be released back into the Earth, let it melt away and down through the soles of your feet back into the Earth. Just as a mother is not harmed by soothing and receiving her children's grief and troubles, Mother Earth is never damaged by your connecting to her like this.

On the sixth inhalation, breathe the energy up to your throat (fifth chakra) and feel it opening this area, which is connected to your voice and to speaking your truth. Then exhale it back down to the Earth.

On the seventh inhalation, breathe the energy up to the middle of your forehead between your eyes (sixth chakra, or third eye) and feel this part of you connected to spiritual vision, higher perception, and intuition, opening and being gently caressed, connected to Mother Earth. Exhale back down into the Earth.

On the eighth and final inhalation, bring the energy all the way up to the top of your head (seventh chakra, or crown) and feel the top of your head opening to spiritual guidance and to light from the cosmos. Feel Mother Earth's energy caressing and opening this area, grounding you between the Earth and sky as a child of Earth and the cosmos. Fill your face, your skull, your brain, your glands, and your hair with this green, nurturing light, connecting you to all of life. On your final exhalation, breathe the energy down your arms and out through your palms, back into Mother Earth. This creates a complete circle of energy. Now you are connected to what is sustaining you in life, what is always there for you. This potent green life force energy can help you heal, revitalize, and balance your whole being.

Practice: Listening to Mother Nature

When I do workshops, we often spend a good hour doing this simple yet powerful practice of listening to Mother Earth. So many of us do not trust our innate ability to speak with, sense, and be taught by Mother Earth. We feel crazy if we listen to what we are hearing from the birds or from a plant. We think we are imagining things. Yet the plants, creatures, trees, stones, and waters are continually speaking to us, giving us messages and information, if only we would tune in and listen. We need to trust the messages and information we are getting from Mother Nature—and know that the living world communicates with us through our feelings. If we can trust what we are feeling when we are open and receptive to Mother Nature, then we can begin to open up to the wisdom, presence, and mysterious depths that are always there for us. The plants and animals and stones want to teach us!

Go outside and find one small thing that calls to you. It can be a particular plant, a stone, a tree, a leaf, a branch, an insect—nothing is too insignificant. Feel what draws your attention and what wants to communicate with you. Sit with that thing for at least fifteen minutes. Pay attention to it. Open to its being, its presence, as fully as you can. This being is alive, just as you are. What does it taste like, smell like, feel like, look like? Rather than thinking about it or studying it in clinical detail, try to feel its life energy. Can you sense its energy in your hand when you touch it or hold it? Does it vibrate fast or slow, and is this vibration smooth or choppy, light or heavy? Is its sound low pitched or high? Can you hear the tone its energy makes? Can you see its color? What gift might it have for you? What might it say to you if it could?

Try to be aware of what impressions, images, and feelings arise as you open to the living energy of the creature of Mother Earth you are with. Do not judge what comes, or yourself. Take note of what comes. You may want to jot down what comes in a journal. Maybe it is a few lines of a poem; maybe you hear a word or a voice, or maybe it says something quite specific to you. What does it say to your spirit? How does it move you? What do you feel when you sit with it, simply paying attention and feeling your heart connection to it?

I am always amazed when people share their experiences of how deep this short practice can be. Some people receive quite a lot of information. Often it is just what they needed to know at that moment, some key to their healing. Other times, it is something about the nature of the plant or being that reveals itself, for the first time, like a revelation. Some people have emotional breakthroughs and find themselves in tears for no apparent reason. Almost everyone feels recharged and refreshed just by taking the attention off himself or herself and giving it to something the person might normally walk past, unnoticed. It can be very healing and balancing to do this. It truly opens the heart and puts us back in relationship to Mother Earth.

It does not take that long to connect to Mother Nature; it only takes a willingness to open up and listen. Because we have been raised in modern society to be extremely rational and logical, there is a tendency to doubt what we feel and what comes to us intuitively or as imagination. Yet what we feel and imagine is as real as what we think—much more so, in fact. The beings of nature connect heart to heart, not on a thinking level. To communicate with the one-legged, the four-legged, the no-leggeds, our brothers and sisters on this living Earth, we must open our hearts and not be afraid to feel *with them*. We must not be afraid to be openhearted, to seem silly, ridiculous, or whimsical to our friends and families for talking to trees, animals, and plants. We must again learn to listen and to relate with intimacy to the children of our Mother Earth, our brothers and sisters all around us, speaking to us and wanting to help us.

Learning to Trust the Unseen:
The Lesson of the Well

From my childhood on, I have had many scrapes with death. Between my physical body being always sick with kidney and heart problems, or injured, and my adventurous (or, some might say, reckless) nature as child who liked to get into dark and mucky places (where the real riches of life are) to look for critters, I have always lived what you might call close to the edge. Whether or not I have wanted to, I have faced many extreme situations and been close to leaving this life many times. A few times, in a moment when I was on the edge between leaving or staying on Earth, a direct intervention from Spirit came in the form a powerful vision or a voice that would speak to me and guide me, quite directly sometimes. One of these guiding voices saved my life and taught me a valuable spiritual lesson about trusting the guidance that we receive, in whatever form it takes, however strange it may seem at the time.

I was about five years old, and it was a usual Sunday. My family had attended church and had gone over to my paternal grandparents' house for dinner, as we always did on Sunday. My father's parents were never exactly kind to me and treated me as the black sheep of the family for some reason I have never understood. Everyone in the family knew of and accepted this state of affairs, so after dinner, I would slip outside and go into the barnyard out back, while everyone else sat around and talked or watched a football game. The barnyard was not much to look at, with its old buildings that had never been taken care of, put together with scrap wood and old fencing materials. It made me sad to see how pitiful the animals' houses were. My grandfather never seemed to have respect for anything, least of all his animals. He treated my siblings and me like he treated his animals when my family lost our home and had to move in with him and my grandmother. Worst of all was when my parents were away. So I was quite happy to get out of his house as soon as I had eaten dinner and could escape. In any case, I loved to explore the many outbuildings and the goat shed and to look for bunnies that had burrowed under them. Every Sunday, I would go exploring and make new discoveries in nature off by myself. Sometimes I went where I knew I shouldn't. This Sunday, I found myself drawn to the old well, which was simply a large mound of dirt up against the west side of the house, built with as little care and pride as the barns had been.

I knew I shouldn't be at the well because we were always told not to go near it. It was so deep and dark that you could easily fall in if you weren't careful. I inched my way up the clay mound that surrounded the well so that I could look in. I peered down the dark hole. As my curiosity grew, I lay in the dirt on my belly so that my head was hanging just over the entrance. The air smelled musty, like damp earth and moss. I tried to let my eyes adjust to the darkness so that I could make out the bottom of the hole. I dropped a few pebbles to hear if there was water, but each time I threw a rock in, all I heard was a thud. Knowing that there was no water down there, my curiosity grew even more about what creatures might be down there—salamanders, water snakes, or maybe even snails. All I knew was that whatever was down there would something I had not seen before. I figured the bottom was probably ten or so feet down. Temptation overcame me, and I decided to venture in.

I ran off to find a makeshift ladder. I remembered that there was an old wooden ladder up against a farm truck behind the haystack, so off I went to fetch it. Slowly I lowered the ladder down the hole, but to my surprise, the ladder wasn't long enough to reach the bottom. I let it drop, figuring that once I lowered my legs down, I could find it with my feet. Slowly I backed my feet and then my legs down the dark hole. I slid my torso along the clay, going further and further into the hole, searching with my feet for the top plank of the ladder. I found myself up to my armpits trying to hold on to the edge the Earth and still not finding a brace for my footing. My arms started to shake and burn as I held on. I tried to pull myself up, but I was too far into the hole for my arms to lift me, and no matter how hard I tried, I could not find the ladder with my feet. Fear began to well up as I realized that I could not pull myself back up and out. If I let go, how far would I fall, and what would be at the bottom? And just how would I get out if I fell in?

It happened slowly, like watching a film in slow motion, as the dirt gave way under my arms and I watched the skyline disappear. I dug my fingers into the dirt as hard as I could, but I was sliding too quickly to stop myself. I fell a good distance, but it was not a straight fall. As I went down, I caught the ladder with my knees, breaking the first three or four rungs. I hit the damp, cold earth, knocking the wind out of me so hard that I thought I would throw up. My jeans were torn at the knees, and I knew I had cut one knee pretty badly. But what was most disturbing was the darkness of the well. I couldn't see anything, not a trace of light. I'm not sure how many feet I had fallen, but it felt like maybe ten or twelve. When I looked up, I couldn't see the sky. I reached down to check my knee and felt the warmth of blood seeping through my jeans. I wasn't sure how bad it was, but I could deal with a cut knee—I was more concerned with how I was going to get out.

The walls were not lined with rock; they were just bare earth. The space I was in was probably about six feet wide. I felt around, running my hands along the walls and trying to grab hold of the thin, twisting roots in the dirt. Every time I tried to climb and find a foothold, I found myself sliding back down the wall. It was cold and damp, a penetrating cold that went right through my small frame. I pulled my arms into my short-sleeved shirt and sat with my back up against the wall of the well, trying to calm myself and think clearly. I tried making a sound, but it was swallowed up, muffled by Earth itself. I realized suddenly how separated I was from anyone or anything above. I knew no one would come looking for me because I often ran off for days at a time. No one would notice I was missing, and if someone did, once I was found, I would surely get in big trouble for venturing near the well.

I went back to trying to climb the dirt walls until my arms simply gave out from exhaustion. Every time, I would slide back down the wall. I sat down and felt the tears starting to come. I remember very clearly wiping the hot tears off my face with the bottom of my T-shirt and feeling the grit of dirt against my cheeks. It seemed like there was more dirt on my T-shirt and hands than on the ground. I was getting frustrated with my situation and was nearing the end of my rope. I was freezing, filthy, hurt, and starting to get really worried that I might not be able to get out. I was stuck in a dark, deep hole with nothing but a broken ladder of rotting wood. I had tried everything I knew to no avail. I knew it must be getting late and that the sun had most likely gone down. My fingers and toes were already numb. I soon found myself kneeling in the bottom of this well with my head bowed and my hands pressed together in prayer, asking for help.

It makes me laugh a little now, looking back on it. I remember being always in some sort of predicament and saying in my prayers, "Dear Heavenly Father . . . ummm . . . it's me again, Kiesha . . ." I would tell him what kind of a fix I had gotten myself into. I must have looked a fright, covered in dirt, with a streaked face and my arms under my shirt, hands pressed together in valiant prayer, with one shoe on and no sock on the other foot because I had tied the sock around my bleeding knee. I prayed, "Heavenly Father, please get me out of this place. Please help me." I was cold, and I didn't like the pitch black, and honestly, I didn't know what to do. I prayed and then sat huddled against the wall.

As I sat in a stupor, picking dirt off my cut and waving my hand back and forth in front of my eyes, trying to see my fingers, I heard her voice calling to me. "Child . . . child, take the wood and dig." I sat still, not answering, not questioning out loud, but thinking to myself, "Dig? I'm in a well for crying out loud—how will digging get me out of this hole?" I thought in my child's way, "I can't possibly dig a tunnel out of here," thinking that that was what I was being told to do. As I sat questioning, I heard again, "Child, take the wood and dig at the wall."

I got on my hands and knees and started to feel around for a piece of broken ladder that was not too big or too small. After a few tries with pieces of wood that broke, I finally found a piece that seemed the right size with which to dig. I held it close to the end and started digging at the layer of earth slightly higher than my head that was softest horizon- tally. The rest of the wall was made up of harder clay and small rocks that chewed at my stick, so I stuck to the soft earth that would crumble at my feet as I worked. I would stop and catch my breath and brush my hair out of my face, letting my arms stop burning before I started again, holding them over my head and digging.

It felt like I was digging forever. The longer I dug and saw no progress, the more frustrated I became. I felt like crying several times and got mad and tossed my stick in anger. Then I had to crawl around and find the thing again. I found myself questioning Her, and then I would feel bad that I was questioning. The minutes had started to feel like hours, and the hours like an eternity. I was exhausted, and my arms burned so badly from digging over my head that I couldn't hold them up any longer. I leaned back on the far wall and put my stick down and started to cry, whimpering, "I can't do it anymore."

Just then, it started to happen. Dirt started to fall in big chunks all around me. I started to panic, thinking I was going to be buried alive in the dirt. I scrambled to the far wall and wedged myself behind an old engine for more protection and cupped my face with my hands to save some air if I was buried alive. Dirt started coming down everywhere—I didn't know how much was coming down, but it was loud, and I could feel clumps of dirt falling on my back and shoulders. When the dirt stopped falling after a few minutes, it was again silent, except for some trickling dirt and rocks. I pulled my hands away from my face and felt around me.

My feet and legs were stuck in dirt up to my knees, and it took a bit of wiggling around to get free from between the wall and the old engine where I had wedged myself. I felt for the wall where I had been digging, and it was not there anymore. A huge mass of earth along the soft ledge I was digging had come down, creating a massive, solid dirt mound inside the well. I found myself scrambling up the huge, soft mound. As I scrambled up to the top, I looked up and, with huge relief, saw the stars! I saw Orion's Belt, my special stars—three of them lined up in a row. I knew by where the stars were in the sky that it was only about eight o'clock.

My first reaction was, "It's only eight?" I was certain that I had been in the hole for the entire night, maybe days, when in reality, it had been about six hours. Seeing the stars, I knew I was going to get out of there. It took a bit of maneuvering, but I finally worked my way up the wall until I felt the brim of the entrance with my fingers. I managed to pull myself up and out of the hole and lay face down in the dirt for a while, out of breath and in amazement. I was out! I did it! I composed myself for a time, then rolled over onto my back, staring up at the stars. The more I thought about what had happened, the more I realized how much help I had received down there.

I was never completely alone; there were larger powers at work that night. They were looking out for me. Maybe they wanted me here? Maybe there was a purpose or a reason for things that I did not yet understand? Though I didn't understand what I was being told, why I had to dig, I had to trust the voice I was hearing. I had to do what was asked of me, without getting wrapped up in figuring out how it could work. I thought I was being asked to dig a tunnel out! I was only asked to dig—to give it my best effort—then the solution appeared. It was a solution that I could not have foreseen. It seemed to go against common sense—but I was thinking inside the box and could not see the other possibilities.

This lesson taught me many things. It taught me about trusting the guidance that comes to us even when it makes no sense or seems illogical. It taught me personally to always listen and to trust in what I am being taught. It also taught me that I have to work wholeheartedly and make an effort toward what I want—only then does the desired goal come within reach, or Divine Providence steps in to help. If I had prayed and all of a sudden a ladder had appeared to help me climb out of that hole, I would not have learned much. Sometimes answers come in a form we do not understand or like, and we have to have faith. Will we disregard the solution, or will we listen to the voice we are hearing that is telling us what we need to do, even if it is far-fetched? Falling down the well taught me to trust and have faith in the guidance coming from Spirit, which often makes no sense, and in the presence and wisdom of that which we cannot see but which constantly surrounds us and is as real as anything we can know with our senses.

To Recognize True Beauty:
The Lesson of the Two Trees

As a child, I learned very directly that Nature holds the key to all life, its meaning and its fulfillment. Mother Nature as a living, breathing life force can and does speak to us, begs us to listen, to see and to understand. Not only does she give us life each and every moment but she gives us the joy we experience within life. Everything she offers is alive and buzzing with energy, love, and excitement. No blade of grass goes unnoticed by her, not one leaf or one grain of sand is uncared for. She is the great Mother of all, and her family is the whole universe. I was taught these things by experience, by being taken care of by her as her child. I was taught through a pure, joyous feeling that all living things are constantly feeling and speaking to one another, and to us. And I was taught by spirits on the other side while I was in her perfect care. Ever since I was about eight years old, I have been spoken to by a voice that has taught me lessons and given me clear and direct information about the universe and the laws of life.

A gentle, patient woman's voice would come that would speak to me and teach me specific lessons about life. I don't know why these lessons came when they did—sometimes they came when I was in dire need. At other times, they came when I was very still and quiet and tuned in to the flow of the natural world. The lessons were very clear and emphatic. The voice would always start by addressing me as "child." If I did not understand, the entire lesson would be repeated. Later, when I was called to be a shaman at age thirty, I was told by a Native American elder that it was the "grandmothers past" who had been speaking to me, that the elders knew I was being taught like this since I was a child. I had never told a living soul about this until I was about twenty-eight, and even then, it was with great anxiety that I shared this about myself.

Being raised a devout Mormon, to admit this—that voices were speaking to me—certainly would have gotten me a direct ticket to hell and damnation. I was not sure myself what to make of this, how to explain it, and whether I might be crazy. I only knew that it made me feel very different from others and that it was best not to speak of it, ever. I will never forget the relief I felt when I was told that someone understood what I had been going through and that there had been a reason for it—knowing that I was not crazy after all!

Among those lessons I was taught, I will never forget one that showed me the nature of true beauty and how to perceive the true value of things. I was just becoming a young woman that summer, when I found myself at my secret spot near the water's edge. I often went there to escape the realities of the physical and sexual abuse that was happening to me at the hands of my two uncles living next door. Wounded deeply, and struggling with my self-worth in the face of such senseless cruelty and humiliation, I hid among the trees and wept. I was feeling very low—worthless and unlovable, to put it mildly. I remember wondering how people could act with such hate and violence. How could someone be so cruel to another person?

All I could think about was how I could never go to heaven now, how I must be unloved by God. Ugly things were happening to me, and I felt I had been made ugly by them. Religion had taught me that even to kiss before marriage was a sin against God and severely punishable. Now, much more had happened to me than a kiss, and the trauma of it was turning over and over in my mind and heart, convincing me I was no longer worthy of God's love or of heaven. And in the Mormon tradition, if you were not worthy of heaven, you were also not worthy of having your family with you after death. My heart was broken, and my self-worth was gone. I was convinced that not only was I ugly or dirty, but I was also unwanted by God.

In my heartache and confusion, I decided to walk toward the field of high grass and pines, where I could hide among the trees. I happened to find the most beautiful tree to sit under. It had the most perfect pine tree shape, and its needles were the most magnificent shade of green. Its smell was intoxicating, and the bark had not a scrape or blemish on it. It seemed to me the most perfect tree. Directly in front of me stood another pine tree that was a bit taller. The bark was deeply gashed where the sap had messily started to seep down the entire length of the trunk. This fact alone repelled me and made me not want to go near it. It looked deformed, scarred from where it had been struck by lightning. I sat there between these two trees, thinking how much more beautiful was the tree under which I sat, and thinking in an unconscious way what an ugly tree the one in front of me was.

Suddenly I got that funny, heavy feeling I get when I am about to receive a teaching from Spirit, so I immediately went inward and prepared myself to receive whatever might come. I waited patiently, and then I heard it: it was a woman's calm, clear voice, the same voice that had spoken to me before. "Child, what do you see?" she asked. "Trees," I answered out loud. "Which of these is the greater tree?" she asked. I answered that the beautiful, perfect tree under which I sat was the greater tree. Wasn't it obvious?

Then I was taught something about that other, ugly tree that I will never forget. The voice told me that the strongest and most important trees in the forest are those that have fought a hard battle and have bravely carried their scars. For a tree to grow strong within its core, it must experience something harsh that puts it in survival mode—a fierce winter, a drought, or a lightning strike. If a tree has been threatened, damaged, broken, or scarred, it will either die or grow on to become one of the strongest trees in the forest. Those trees that have made it through a battle, that have lived in survival mode longer than the others, produce not only the most seeds but the most dominant and strong seeds. Those pine trees that have weathered much send all their life energy into their pine cones—and these are the trees that repopulate the whole forest, ensuring its continuance.

Hours went by as I sat there, thinking about what I was being told. I was then asked again by the voice, "Which is the greater tree?" My answer this time was very different, and my chest burned and tears welled up in my eyes as I answered that it was the so-called ugly tree in front of me that was the greater one. The most strong, glorious, and beautiful tree was the one that had survived much and that bore the scars of its struggles and battles. It became capable of a vast amount of regeneration and the giving of new life. Once the lesson was over and I was sure the voice was not going to return, I sat at the water's edge and looked into my reflection. There sat a girl with a broken spirit and with tears streaming down her face. I really looked at myself. Perhaps, like the tree, I, too, was not as ugly as I thought. I pulled the hood of my green sweatshirt up over my head and started for home.

Thinking back on this lesson now, as an adult, I see how important this is to understand on a deep level, how it applies to so much in our lives. How many of us carry scars that we would rather not carry and feel damaged by what we have experienced throughout our lives? How many of us regret our past hardships, the pain we have experienced and still experience, wishing it would go away? How many of us feel that we are not beautiful or loveable, or that we are intrinsically flawed? I struggled with this feeling as a child, and I still do. I think we all do. I felt that something must be terribly wrong with me because I wasn't really loved or protected as a child. I could not understand what had marked me for such treatment, such hardship. I made the assumption, as any abused child would, that God must not love me, that I was not worthy of love and protection. My religious training supported this view: that we human beings are intrinsically sinful and bad and must earn our entrance into heaven by being near-perfect, unblemished, and pure beings. These religious values are contrary to life itself and do much damage to people. This way of thinking could not be further from the truth. Yet, as a child, I was taught to think this way.

What I learned from the two trees is that it is our wounds that make us strong. Our imperfections are signs of what we have had to struggle with to survive, markers of what we have lived through and learned on our journey. What we have suffered can make us wiser, more understanding, more compassionate, and stronger. The soul can never be wounded. Only our idea of who we are carries the wound. Rather than feeling blemished or tarnished by what we have been through, we can claim our scars and know that the greatest beauty is found beneath the surface of things, when we look deeply. True beauty and goodness cannot be judged from the surface of things—it takes deep listening and seeing. We seldom ever see the value of who we are or our own beauty. Others may see it, but we often cannot. For most of us, it is a lifelong commitment to really love ourselves and accept the gifts that our struggles and pain have given us.

In my own healing journey, in my late twenties, I finally had the courage to share with others some of the things I have been through in my life. I will never forget a line that my dearest friend wrote to me at that time. I carry it with me, and it was essential in helping me become reconciled with my past and understand the gifts my suffering has given to me. The simple statement was, "The wound is where the light gets in."

We may struggle for years with the question of why something had to happen to us and what purpose it could possibly have served, especially when we lost something in the process. Though I think that healing from abuse is a lifelong process, I can see that just by surviving and making a commitment to living and being a loving person, a tremendous amount of light was opened in my life. My hardships put me at the very edge of life and death, and veils were torn away in the process. Because I was so open and in need of help, Mother Earth stepped in and blanketed me in her Love. Spirit stepped in and taught me so that I could stay here, so that I could live and continue on. As many of us already sense, it is often through extreme adversity that we are opened to spiritual blessings and deeper vision. Though I still sometimes struggle with the question of why I had such a difficult childhood, I know that my purpose in speaking to you now is directly tied to those things I learned as a child out in the wilderness. It is also, in some mysterious way, tied to the painful things that drove me to the wilderness and into the arms of the great Mystery.

Confronting the Fear of the Unknown: A Lesson in the Night

Just as I learned the lesson of the two trees from the familiar voice that spoke to me as a child, I was taught many such spiritual lessons over the course of my childhood. In fact, I am still being taught, though now, the lessons come in different forms such as visions and images that I see as a picture screen that opens, not just through a clear voice that speaks to me. In the past, these spoken teachings often came at times when I needed them most. One unforgettable lesson came when I was in extreme duress and terrified. It taught me something huge about the nature of fear.

It was late July, and the grass was at its highest down by the river, reaching my waist. I had run to my special spot in the wilderness as fast as my legs could take me. I emptied my pack and laid out the items I always had with me: my pocketknife, my hoodie, my lighter. Since evening was coming on, I decided to start gathering wood to burn for my fire that night. I wandered around the brush until I had gathered enough wood to last me the night, then made a fire pit from the old volcanic rock that was prominent in that area. Darkness came quickly, but I didn't mind at all. I always liked being surrounded by the dark and watching the fire. It felt to me like an embrace of sorts, as if the world were not so big in the dark (the opposite of how many people feel about the dark, I suppose!).

That night, I was so consumed with my thoughts and with replaying the day's events repeatedly in my mind that I hadn't noticed how severe the windstorm was that had blown in. I pressed my body more firmly against the tree trunk and huddled into my bed of soft, newly grown chico brush. I stoked the fire and had just hunkered down for the night when I heard a sound that instantly raised the hair on the back of my neck.

It sounded like a woman's blood-curdling scream. I had never heard anything quite like it and couldn't place it. I was terrified. It was a new experience for me to be afraid outdoors. Outdoors was where I usually felt safest—I could relate with nature better than I could with people. I sat up quickly and pressed my body against a tree trunk, trying to focus my eyes on anything out in the darkness past my dwindling fire. I remember straining to hear the cry again, trying to filter out the sound of the wind that blew through the trees. As I sat very still, trying to make some sort of sense out of what I was hearing, I realized that I could not feel what it was and had no recollection of the sound. The more I realized that I didn't know what I was dealing with, the more frightened I became. I put more wood and brush on the fire to try to light up the surrounding area, and then I heard it again. The blood-curdling scream was so loud and powerful that my mind ran wild with images of what might be happening across the valley. I was certain that a woman was being hurt or killed nearby. Something horrible was happening, and I didn't know what to do. Should I go and try to help? Would I be killed, too?

My trembling hands dug frantically in the dirt trying to find anything with which I could protect myself. Finally, I found a half-buried fence post. I scrambled back to my tree with my fence post as a weapon and searched the night, while the shrieking screams continued intermittently. I truly couldn't remember ever being so scared and feeling so helpless there in the dark, ready to strike at anything that came near me. I could feel my heart pounding in my chest against my jacket, and soon, hot tears started to streak my dirty face.

Then, all of a sudden, like so many times before, a feeling of heaviness and warmth came over my body, and I heard the familiar voice of Spirit. It came as it always did: peaceful, pleasant, and calming. The voice clearly and gently asked, "Child, why are you afraid?"

I lowered my stick a little and said, "That sound—I am afraid of that sound!" There was a moment of silence then, and in my terrified state, I yelled out, "Come back!" The soft voice came again, assuring me that she was with me. She asked again, "Child, tell me, why are you afraid?" I tried slowing my breathing and pulled my knees up to my chest, knowing that I needed to think about my answer. I said shakily, "I'm scared because I don't know what is happening or what that sound is."

She told me then that the sound I was hearing was the sound of two mountain lions mating on the other side of the meadow. My whole body relaxed instantly, and the fear evaporated, just like that. The lesson continued, and I learned much more. I was taught that we are only afraid of what we do not know; we only strike out at that which we do not understand. Once I knew exactly what and where the sounds were coming from, I was asked again, "Child, are you afraid?" Of course, I smirked and shook my head no. Once I knew it was animals doing something very natural, I knew I had nothing at all to be afraid of.

On this night, the voice spoke to me an extended lesson. It seemed to go on for an hour or more, and its message was imprinted most powerfully on me because of my heightened emotions. It spoke of how fear of the unknown has caused human beings to judge and persecute each other and to strike out against each other since time immemorial. It emphasized how human beings must understand how our initial reactions to that with which we are unfamiliar are often violent and aggressive. It showed me how I was so afraid that night, and so ready to strike out, that I could not think calmly or rationally—and how, once I understood the nature of the sound, I was no longer afraid of it.

Thinking back on this lesson as an adult, and why it was given so pointedly and in such specific detail, it seems that Spirit really wanted me to deeply understand that we are often afraid only because we do not understand something—that we are all the children of one Mother, more the same than different, more deeply recognizable to each other than unknown. My frightening experience was thankfully interrupted by help from the spirit world, as if I had been woken from a nightmare, as if a shadow on the wall had been unmasked by flicking on the light switch. Maybe all our fears and terrors are like that—not quite as real as we think, when we open to the light of Spirit and take time to understand with our hearts that which is unfamiliar and unknown.

In the Wilderness of Despair, a Reason to Live

In every life, there are major events that change the person's destiny. In a family, there can also be major events that change everyone's life for better or for worse. I do not tell the following story to shock you or emphasize my own personal trials but rather in the hope that this story may help other young people and show how facing severe adversity when we are young can make us that much stronger and more open to the blessings of Spirit later. In my family, the event that changed all our lives for the worse was my father losing his sheep ranch when I was five years old.

Our whole childhood, we were extremely poor. It is hard for most people to imagine that a family of seven could live on eleven thousand dollars a year in America, but that's what we did for many years. My father was a farmer and ranch hand and had never known anything else. My great grandfather helped found this tiny, remote Mormon community in Colorado, coming by covered wagon across the Great Plains. Since those first hardy pioneers settled here, we had been people of the land. With few jobs other than those in farming and ranching available and only a high school education, my father did what he knew how to do and did his best to provide. When I was about three years old, he had finally scraped and saved up to buy a humble farm on the outskirts of a little town called "Blanca," which is at the foot of Mount Blanca, one of the highest mountains in Colorado. He spent his last dollar buying the lambs needed to start the ranch. He was planning to start his own small farm and raise his family on this beautiful land, but then the unimaginable happened.

One night, someone snuck onto our land and, in the midst of the darkness, loaded most of the sheep and lambs into a trailer and took off. With one action, my father's plans and dreams for the farm were crushed. Our family was crushed. There was no backup, no savings, no insurance. We lost the house and became homeless, just like that. I remember having to load up all our belongings into a pickup truck. All five of us children held on to different household items as we sat in the back of an old pickup truck and drove down the dirt road, having to leave our home, not knowing exactly where we would go or what we would do.

I cannot even imagine how my parents must have felt, having five children, nowhere to go, not a dime to their name, and no home to call their own. To add to the difficulty, four of my siblings have some form of disability—they were born with a genetic syndrome called "fragile X," which is similar to Down's syndrome, but without the facial characteristics. In my two brothers, it is more severe (as it usually is in males), whereas in my sisters, it is slight and more comparable to a learning disability. Though my brothers are both in their twenties now, developmentally, they are still about ten years old and truly innocent angels. So for much of my childhood, my family had quite a struggle just to survive in a basic way.

We ate potatoes for breakfast, lunch, and dinner for months on end at times. When things were hardest, I can remember my mother passing around a stalk of celery so that each of us kids could have one bite apiece. We were often hungry. Living in a rural religious farming community, people hid their poverty and needs out of pride. Not being able to take care of one's own family was shameful, and we did not ask for handouts. Going on welfare was shameful, too, and though it did eventually come to this, I remember my mother's shame at having to use food stamps. We would shop for food in another town so as not to be seen using them. Yet we were desperate.

This desperation caused us to move in with my father's parents. It was to be a temporary situation. My father had plans to build us a house from scratch, adding to it little by little, while buying every plank and nail with whatever money he had. Unfortunately, this would take time—years, in fact. In the meantime, we were stuck living as charity cases at my grandparents' house. The years we spent living there were not good for any of us. The memories of that time are among the worst I have, and it was during this time that many horrendous things happened to me and to my siblings. My grandfather treated my mother and brothers and sisters as if we were beggars off the street. My mother was on pins and needles the entire time, never knowing if she was going to do something wrong in that house. She tried to keep quiet and out of the way, while keeping us children out of the way as much as possible, too. The seven of us stayed in one room, sharing two large beds. Knowing that we were always going to be in trouble for something, we tried to be invisible, but nothing was enough. My grandfather made it clear that we were resented and treated us like dogs.

He was a low-class kind of person, one who beat his animals, who gossiped and complained about everyone, and who did only the amount of work he had to and spent money as fast as he earned it. He had no appreciation for schooling or anything other than his own shallow existence. He was one of those people who lived without dignity, and everything on his property was junked up, run down, or shabbily constructed. There was no pride taken in anything. The term *white trash* was pretty fitting. Picture a leaning house with a porch made entirely of old screened doors fastened together with nails, screws, duct tape, and bailing twine. The barn and sheds were never cleaned out, and the manure had piled up so high that you would be standing in several feet of the stuff inside the sheds. And these sheds were filled with old TVs, radios, and washing machines. The poor animals lived among it all. Even the yard of my grandparents' house was a junkyard, filled with hundreds of old washing machines, dryers, refrigerators, and car parts. My grandfather's answer for how he lived was always to say, "It's good enough for who it's for." This lack of dignity and respect for anything had nothing to do with being poor. It was a spiritual condition, and unfortunately, we all suffered because of it.

We children would be scolded for eating anything in the house—and when they did give us something to eat, it was bread with mayonnaise, ketchup, and mustard on it. If we were thirsty, all we got to drink was goat's milk from the barn. To this day, the smell of goat's milk or cheese turns my stomach. At night, my brothers and sisters and I would lie in bed, our stomachs growling, while hearing my grandparents eating popcorn, chips, and goodies that they hid from us and never allowed us to eat. I remember feeling sick with rage knowing that my sweet and innocent brothers were awake at night and listening to my grandparents munching away, their stomachs growling. I remember my one brother going to the fridge to look for food and getting spanked and belittled. *Hate* is a strong word, but I hated how they treated us.

Then things went from bad to worse. My sister Kelsy got very sick and had to have open-heart surgery. My parents had to take her to the children's hospital in Denver for endless testing and, later, for several surgeries. They would be gone for weeks on end, living at the Ronald McDonald House there, just trying to save my poor sister's life. It was hard for my brothers and sisters who were left behind with the relatives, but it must have been hell for my parents, too, who were sick with worry over their daughter who was dying and for their children left alone with unkind relatives. The open-heart surgery did not go as well as planned, and my sister had to stay in the intensive care unit at the hospital for three months. My parents struggled just to feed themselves each day and pay expenses while my sister hung on between life and death. Eventually she pulled through and was able to come home with my parents. In the meantime, it seemed like my parents were gone forever, and we kids were left to fend for ourselves. During these times when my parents were gone, we truly were at the mercy of our relatives. Some of them crossed the line from simple cruelty to downright criminality.

My father was a decent, hardworking, respectable man, but some of his siblings were not. They apparently inherited their father's sadism, meanness, and worse. It was during this time that I started being abused by my uncle who lived down the street. He would tie me up to the barn and whip me, getting a twisted pleasure out of seeing me in pain. Soon after, my other uncle began sexually taunting and abusing me. This despised uncle was always there watching me. When I would walk to my great grandmother's house, whom I loved more than life, he would be across the street watching me. If I went into the field behind my house, he would be watching me. I began to feel like hunted prey, always afraid of when I would be hurt next and in a constant state of fear and anxiety. I realized that I could not trust the adults around me.

Between the cruelty of my grandfather and the sadism of my two uncles, I just wanted to disappear. The only adult with whom I felt safe was my great grandmother. Indeed, one of the only people who seemed to care for me or treat me with any tenderness at all was my great grandmother, whom I called "Grandma Jensen." She was an old-fashioned, strong-willed, spiritual, somewhat stern, yet very loving woman. She was the only adult who existed for me at that time, and I would even sleep under her bedroom window at night just to be close to her. Though we had a special connection, she could not protect me from what was going on, and I never told her, not wanting to break her heart. These were her own children and grandchildren doing these awful things. I learned to run away and to find safety in nature, in the wilderness, where no one could find me. But as a child, my will to live was slowly being eroded because it seemed that so many adults in my life were set on mistreating and abusing me.

It pains me now to think of it, how numb and terrified I was as a child and how alone I was much of the time. I picture myself as I often was, sitting in the old apple tree next to my great grandmother's house, or behind the old chicken coop, my face dirty, my hair uncombed and matted, usually nursing some wound I had received from one of the adults in my life. My eyes were hollow, and I was between terror and numbness most of the time. The only time I was truly happy was when I was playing with the animals or exploring by myself in nature. Looking back, it seems amazing that I made it to adulthood at all. I never thought about what I would be when I grew up. I never thought I would make it to adulthood. Since I have had my own children and have done my utmost to ensure that they are safe, loved, and cared for, I have come to realize just how intense and desperate my situation was as a child. Why no one seemed to notice what was going on or ever intervened when there were such clear signs of abuse and neglect is beyond me.

But no memory is more painful to me than the day when I decided I had had enough. I had just been taunted and humiliated by my uncle, who had torn my bathing suit off—I had managed to escape and run away to hide in an old barn among my grandfather's corrals. I sat there in a complete daze, having been wounded, embarrassed, exposed, and terrified. The only solution that I could see was to leave the family, to leave this place forever. I did not fit in. I was openly hated by my father's family, tortured by them; I felt invisible and was neglected. I couldn't even cry—I had moved into a place of hopelessness, numbness, and emptiness that no child should ever feel.

The dust was piled up thick on everything. There was an old goat skin hanging on one wall and a large barrel filled with grain on the other, some horse tack hanging on the walls near the door, and some old rope lying on a dingy green trunk on the floor, in which old, homemade jars of canned vegetables were stored. My eyes were fixed on the old rope. I knew what I had to do. The rope was old but strong, and as I drew it up and through my hands, making a careful noose, little trails of the coarse rope splintered into my palm.

I was sure there was no other way. I couldn't think beyond it this time. I was simply going to go away. Away from my father's family who disgusted and pained me, who hurt me and made me afraid. Away from the other school kids, the girls with whom I just couldn't fit in and the boys who, for some reason, looked at me differently, even though I felt and acted like one of them. Just away! I gathered up the rope and climbed up the side of the barn until I got to the beam. Slowly I tied the rope around the wooden frame, and the other end I pulled over my head and rested on my collarbones. This life was going to be over soon, and then everything would be green again, like Earth in the spring after a crisp rain.

My bare feet slid to the edge of the beam, which was thick with years of dust, and my toes curled and clutched the edge. I closed my eyes and leaned forward, throwing myself off balance, and in that split second between life and escape, I heard something that made my heart go cold and my body seize with panic. It was this soft and familiar voice calling my name. It was my younger brother Kent! I caught myself from falling with my hands, scrambling on the rough-cut lumber on the facing wall, scraping myself to stop. My hands were bleeding, huge wood splinters gouged deep into my palms, as I pressed my feet as hard as I could to the beam, holding myself horizontally. I heard his little voice again. I watched through the slats as he came closer and closer. I started to cry and pray at the same time, begging the Lord that the barn door would not open. I could not let him see this! His little voice, coming closer, was calling, "Kieshaaaa!"

My muscles were shaking in exhaustion, and my hands felt as if they had caught fire as the blood dripped down the wall, but all I focused on was the little shadow moving in front of the barn. If I fell, he would hear the noise and see his sister hanging from a noose, and if he opened the door now, he would see a sight nearly as bad. I watched his little passing shadow walk quietly away while I tore my hand from the wall and reached for the rope that was snug against my neck. The rope that I had hoped would take me away was now the very thing that was saving my life. Hand over hand, I used the rope to pull myself back upright onto the beam, and there I sat. All I could think about was how selfish I was and how God must have been ashamed of me. The thought of my brother Kent being without me, or finding me in such a state, made me sick. My stomach cramped, and I buckled over and vomited again and again from sheer panic.

I climbed down quickly, wiped my mouth on my shirt, and shoved my bleeding hands into my pockets, squeezing the material to soak up the blood as I ran to my brother, who was now in tears trying to find me. I called his name and ran to him and fell on my knees when I reached him. I held him so tight and sobbed, while he told me again and again, "I couldn't find you, and I couldn't find you . . ."

This day, this horrible and momentous day, is etched in my mind forever, reminding me of how precious life is. I felt that if there were only one reason for me to stay on this Earth, in this family, it was to be a loving protector for my siblings. I lay in bed that night with my precious Kent snuggled up beside me, his soft breath against my neck as I held him tight. There are days when one can fix one's gaze on the sun itself without being blinded—and this is how I saw him. I was dazzled, entranced, and I felt grateful to him with my whole being. I vowed to live my life for him, for my other brother, and for my sisters. I knew without question that they were the reason I was born. This small boy needed me, and I needed him. This day impressed me with such a lesson, a lesson of greater love, selflessness, and the value of human tenderness. It didn't matter what would come and trample me, what thunderstorms would come, or what hideous abuse I might face; I would stand strong and brave and become a gentler, more compassionate and loving person. I thought that perhaps this was the reason terrible things were happening to me, to save my siblings from them. This gave me strength to face things; it gave me a purpose. Though I could not protect myself, I would fight with my last breath protecting my brothers and sisters from harm. It became my life's goal, to make sure they never felt that pain from my uncles, never felt the severity of that wrath or that corruption of innocence. As a child, I honestly believed that I could keep them from harm.

I write as if my world changed in this moment. It didn't, but the way I thought about my world did. I started to see in life a greater beauty, to see life as a gift, although the beatings and abuse still came. I still ran. I ran to the fields or to the corrals. I would lose myself searching for creatures and then watch them for hours on end, just listening to what stories they had to tell. I would climb the trees and stay for hours, day and night, swinging in the branches, listening to the leaves rustling in the wind. Nature became my best teacher and always gave me answers in subtle ways. I learned that if I held still long enough and really looked, the world was alive, living, breathing, and in a constant dance.

One thing this painful, near-tragic experience taught me was that when life is unbearable, living for others and seeing how necessary we are to them can be life saving. The love we receive and give to others can be life saving, and even when we suffer terribly from hatred and abuse, there is a part of us that cannot be conquered—that part of us that wants to see the beauty of life; it can receive that beauty, and it wants to live! And that aspect is capable of a vast and giving love, even if we were never loved ourselves. I decided that day to live for love, to not let go of life. It was love that kept me here, and it is love that keeps me here now, despite the many formidable challenges I have faced since.

Kindling the Light of Spirit in Children

Young people today face so much suffering at a young age. There is so much abuse, so much instability and chaos, so much abandonment by adults. This disintegration of the social fabric is part of the age in which we live and part of the death that we have been collectively undergoing. It is part of what makes massive evolutionary change inevitable, because we cannot go on this way for much longer. There is a sickness in the heart of humanity, just as Nature is sick. The children today are just as threatened as is Nature herself by humanity's materialism, which emphasizes personal gratification and loss of spiritual values. My heart goes out to young people today who are struggling just to survive, to grow up healthy, who do not know what they are worth and who are confronted by meaninglessness. Many are in danger of being lost, unless they can tap into a source of nourishment that is much bigger than their families, their identities, and their environments. They need, above all, to connect to their own higher selves—to Spirit and the life-giving waters that are always there within them.

To those young people, I say with all my heart, hang on; never let go or give up on your precious life. You are so very special. You have a larger purpose than you can ever realize. You make a difference here, and whether anyone else around you knows it or not, you are a divine spark who can do anything with your life, who can create whatever you want from this life. Someday you may be amazed to find where your life has led you and what you have become.

Stay true to your own heart, whatever comes. The love in your heart and the light of your being cannot be diminished by anyone or anything. I could never have imagined where my life would take me and that I would one day change from feeling invisible, unlovable, and helpless to remembering the larger purpose for which my soul came here. I never imagined things could be different—amazingly beautiful and joyous. In this life, anything can happen. Be patient, and know that all the love you wish for, all the freedom to be who you really are, is coming. You can do amazing things with your vision and your light. Going through something extreme or painful can give you huge gifts—and make you strong enough to carry out a very large purpose in life, to affect others even more powerfully.

We are not the things that happen to us or the mistakes we've made. We are not victims. We are not our families. Your soul comes from divine light and love. Your soul, your own higher self, is the sovereign of your being, and nothing can stain or diminish it. Inside, you are utterly free and can choose how you will experience this life. If your family or surroundings do not support you, you can still stay true to that highest love and light within you, hold to a higher way of being. When things get tough, hang on—and know that your life has infinite meaning and value, that *you* are so amazingly precious and needed here. Mother

Earth needs you. The world needs the light you bring just by being you!

The young people here today have a huge role to play in changing this world. They will be the first ones to start living from the heart and will actually guide the adults when the time comes. They will lead us back into the heart. By trusting their own souls, they will be the first to know what it is to live as Love. We must do everything we can to help them and protect them, these great beings who are now incarnate on Earth as our children. Most of all, we must listen to them, pay attention to them. As parents and adults, we can support them in connecting with their higher selves, in opening to their own guidance from the spirit world and Great Spirit. We can give them the experience of nature, help them form a living relationship with Mother Earth. Their beings are so sensitive that this early exposure will have vast effect. While the adults living today who came here to help support the great shifting of consciousness on planet Earth will face challenges and will know the dying away as well as the birthing, the children will inherit a changed world. They will give shape to the future of humanity by living from their hearts. The children will remember the way before anyone else. They are here to lead humanity to the next stage in its development.

I have often wondered if maybe the purpose of children's suffering is to cause them to connect to their higher selves, as a matter of survival and spiritual strengthening. The gift of a difficult childhood can be that you find your courage and inner strength early on and decide what in life is most important. Though no child should have to experience suffering, it is a great mystery how we are shaped and molded by adversity and how our souls may have chosen certain experiences for exactly this purpose—to grow and become who we are meant to become. Our children are our greatest gift and responsibility—we must nurture their spirits and give them the life-giving nutrients they need as much as we can, so that when the time comes, they will lead us in becoming Love.

After a Great Loss, a Redeeming Vision

I mentioned earlier that my great grandmother, Grandma Jensen, was the most beloved person in the world to me, a woman whose tenderness was so important when I was a child. She was already in her eighties when I was growing up. She had helped settle this small Mormon community with her husband back in the early 1900s. She was the matriarch of the family, having raised five children herself after her husband died, at a time when a woman needed a man with her even to buy lumber. She was a devout and strong woman with a heart of gold. I used to spend hours and hours up in her apple tree, where I was hidden from everyone's view but hers. She would stand at her kitchen window watching me trying to stay out of view, but when I would wave, she would always step closer to the window and wave back. I always knew she was there.

If my brothers and sisters owned my heart, she owned my soul. How I loved every word she spoke, every gray hair and wrinkle, every glance she gave me! She soothed me and somehow made living sweet, even when it was otherwise very rough. As an adult, I have noticed that whenever I love something, it is because it reminds me of her. From the taste of a homemade waffle to the smell of lilacs and sweet peas, so many things invoke the memory of Grandma Jensen. As I would come through the door, she would say, "I was just thinking about you. Let's have some pop." Then she would pour Dr. Pepper into two small pixie cups and hand me a Little Debbie cookie as we sat at the kitchen table and talked about this or that. No matter what she had to say, it was like honey to my ears. Everything she said seemed profound and wise. We would sip our pop and she would tell me stories of the two world wars or the Great Depression, of working the sheep for Papa and driving the wagon team down from the hills. She would tell me of being a child and gathering eggs to trade for her lunch at the old schoolhouse, trying tobacco for the first time, and going to the first picture show back in the day. When I had trouble in school or had been punished unfairly, she would go down to the school and stand up for me. When I was given a really unpleasant chore that she knew I hated, such as plucking chickens, she would help me. She was always looking out for me in little ways.

I started to stay the nights with her, sleeping in her perfectly kept living room on the couch. I never wanted to leave her side. She was getting older, and I couldn't sleep unless I was close to her, knowing she was okay. She was not the only one getting older—so was I. Soon I'd be sixteen, and nothing much mattered to me other than my great grandmother. I started to sneak out at night and take my pillow and blankets from the couch to the hallway floor, scared I wouldn't be able to hear her well enough if she needed me. And then one night, long after the stars and the moon had come out, I heard her calling my name.

I jumped up and listened again to make sure I wasn't just dreaming, and I heard her again. I was at her bedside in a flash. I found her sitting on the edge of the mattress with her frail, bent fingers tucked into her lap. She patted the bed and looked at me a few moments, and then pressed her palm to my face as only she ever did. I tried to read her face and tell what was the matter. She calmly said, "Shhhh, I'm fine. I want to tell you something that will be hard to hear." I didn't know what to expect, but I knew by the look of concern on her face that it wasn't good. She stroked my face and whispered, "Oh, Kiesha, I love you," and I told her I loved her back, reaching up and cupping her hand. She told me not to be afraid of what she was going to tell me, because she was at ease with it. I nodded, and she proceeded to tell me about the visitation she'd had that night.

"Momma and Papa and my brother Reece came to see me tonight. They stood right there at the end of the bed and woke me from my sleep. They said I would be coming home to be with them very soon." She stopped and studied my face in silence for a while. I was unable to speak or move, since the lump in my throat was burning and aching so fiercely that I dared not open my mouth. She told me she wasn't afraid, that she would be happy to go back home. She missed her family, and she would be fine.

I was panicked—she couldn't leave me! What would I do without her? How could I survive? I ate breakfast with her every morning before school, I slept with her at night, I prayed for her every night and slept under her window as a child in the rain, snow, and summer storms just to be near her—and she was going to leave me? My face must have said it all. She pulled me onto her chest and whispered, "It will be okay. You will be okay!" That night, I lay beside her in her bed. She held my hand, and in the dark, I whispered, "I love you, Grandma," and she whispered it back, her voice cracking with emotion.

In the morning, I was awakened by her getting up and sitting at the edge of the bed, pulling open the bottom drawer to her dresser. I sat up with interest. I knew every inch of that house, but never did I know what was in that bottom drawer because it was never opened. I sat next to her, and she slid the heavy dresser drawer open and showed me a picture of my great grandfather Earl before he had passed away. She held it to her chest before handing it to me, then she dug a little deeper into the drawer and pulled out some things that she had been saving, things that were precious to her. She placed these items in my hands and made me give her my word that I would keep them safe and that I would never sell them or give them to anyone else in the family. She said she knew "they would look for them." I tucked these precious few items into my bag and took them straight home to my hiding place with a bit of happiness that she had chosen me to keep them and a deep sadness knowing that she was certain she would be leaving this world.

It was a few days later when she fell and had to be taken to the hospital. I knew what was happening. I knew she was going to be leaving. I couldn't bear it. I walked down the hospital hallway under the buzzing overhead lights in a daze. One of the nurses called my name and walked toward me, hugged me briefly, and took my hand to lead me to my great grandmother's room. There she was, looking so thin under that white knit blanket. Her crooked fingers waved me over, and I rested my head in her lap. This was more painful for me than any injury, any embarrassment, or any humiliation. This was unbearable. I was dying from the inside out, and nothing could stop it from happening. I lay there with her, never leaving her side. I refused to go to school. If she didn't eat, I didn't eat; if she didn't sleep, I didn't sleep. I think we both knew it was going to happen soon. I remember looking at her with tears rolling down my face and whispering to her how much I loved her. Her eyes filled up and spilled over, but she could not talk. She just looked at me and silently said everything she needed to. And then she was gone.

I was sure my heart would stop. In a way, my heart did stop. Nothing could console me. Nothing could make the hurt go away. I lived in the apple tree for days. I couldn't bear the sight of food, and sleep seemed never to come. I would watch my brothers Kent and Kort from the tree in the backyard playing, then lie back down in the limbs and stare into the leaves. I'm not sure what I even thought about. There was a numbness inside me that seemed as large as consciousness itself. Soon after my great grandmother died, my kidneys began to fail. I have heard that the kidneys emotionally relate to grief and can be impacted by strong grief. If so, mine were drained and depleted, so great was my loss. It was the greatest loss I had ever suffered—to lose the one person whom I treasured above all else. My lifeline was gone.

All I could think about was how to get to where she was. My will to live was once more hanging by a thread. And then I had a dream, a dream so powerful that I know it was actually more of a vision. I have had this recurring vision several times in my life, always when I am in a desolate place or facing some major turning point. In it is the key to my past, to my future, and to the purpose for which my soul came here.

In the vision I saw a massive oak tree standing dead at the top of a huge hill in the distance. Then I was shown a small valley full of thorny brush laden heavy with ripe red berries. I was told to follow the dirt path until I reached the base of the valley, and there I was to gather all the ripened fruit until every last bush was harvested. The work was so very hard. I could feel the heat of the sun burning my skin, the stinging of my arms and hands where the thorns had cut deep gashes into my skin, and my clothes were nothing but tattered and torn rags. When my wooden barrel was full of the berries, I would dump them into a huge tub again and again, until all the fruit was picked and the tub was full. Then I was instructed to stomp the berries into juice with my bare feet. My legs and my arms all the way up to my elbows were dyed a dark red by the time I was finished. I knew then that I had to haul the juice up to the top of the huge hill where the dead tree stood and pour it all the way around the tree's trunk.

This part of the vision was the hardest—the struggle up the hill carrying the weight of the juice in huge buckets. My arms and shoulders burned, my legs trembled, and it took every ounce of my strength to make it to the top of the great hill. Once I had poured this dark red juice around the tree's trunk, I stood back and waited for something to happen. All at once, one of the huge limbs from the tree broke off the trunk and fell to the Earth with a great thud, one end of the limb becoming rammed deep into the ground. After a moment or two, I watched with amazement as something wonderful started to happen: the limb started to grow little green leaves and to branch out of itself—it was growing green again, full of life!

When I awoke from this vision, I was in an altered state. It was so potent that I was trembling and sweating and felt as if I would float. I felt as if I would never sleep again. Something in this vision made me understand that I had to continue on. Although I didn't understand the meaning of the dream just yet, I knew that I had something to do in this life and that it was important.

Whenever it has come to me, unbidden, always the same, the vision's strong symbolism and mystery tell me powerfully that new life can come from what is dead—that I can make a difference if I keep working, keep struggling on, despite everything. Though this vision may relate to my specific karma or path in this life, I think it applies to the human experience, too. This journey through life is not easy—we do not get through it without bruises and scars. Yet perhaps we are here to heal and renew what is dead in our family line, our culture, our planet, ourselves, through our relentless love, effort, and spiritual commitment. Perhaps we have a greater purpose than we ever can imagine in coming here to Earth and into these particular families and communities and bodies. Our existence and what we do while we are here deeply matters to the rest of existence. I know that those of us who are here now on planet Earth are here to be the bringers of new life—that this will not be easy but that it is why we chose to be here, during this time of great transformation, dying, and rebirth

And so we must keep walking up that hill, struggling on, learning, and gathering and pouring the juice of life, loving life and each other as much as we can. This kind of love requires all our faith and courage. Through Love, I pray that what has withered and died can grow green again; through Love, I pray that Mother Earth and each one of us can be brought back to life, our tender shoots and buds rising up out of dead limbs toward the sky.

Lessons from Nature

Before I knew anything about shamanism, I lived for the animals, nature, trees, mountains, and streams. My life just naturally became focused in that direction from the earliest age. I have known how to interact and speak with animals since I was a very small girl. Later I made it my business to learn everything I could about them—their biology, habits, natures. I read *National Geographic* and animal books with a passion, memorizing facts about as many animals as I could. But mostly, I studied the animals around me and spent time around them whenever I could. Eventually I became a wildlife specialist and got involved with animal rehabilitation and rescue in the area where I grew up, often working with the Bureau of Land Management and different wildlife organizations. I would help when someone's cows or sheep or horses fell ill or had been attacked by a mountain lion or when an animal or bird was found injured on public land. In truth, it was all I cared about growing up, and I spent most of my life outdoors, studying nature and learning from her. Mother Nature has taught me many things over the years such as how to interact with and respect the creatures and how to appreciate the love that is all around us, flowing through every single act of nature.

Gathering Honey with the Bees

If any creature deserves our respect, it is the bee. Bees are truly one of the most sacred gifts to creation. What they do for us in pollinating the flowers and plants, in giving us honey and perfect, complete healing substances created from their own beautiful bodies, is truly amazing. They are one of the most important creatures in the life cycle of planet Earth—yet we often forget just how much we owe to them, how much we depend on them for our survival.

Bees pollinate over one hundred different crops in America alone.

Without their daily dedication to pollinating flowers, we would not have fruit, vegetables, nuts, or berries. There are over twenty thousand different species of bee, and every one of them is crucial to the planet's ecosystems. Without the bee, the web of life on planet Earth would fail. Such a small creature does so much for our planet and yet is so overlooked most of the time. Bees make our Earth life more abundant, fruitful, and sweet—literally. They are one of the species that has been mysteriously disappearing over the last few years, and no one knows why or how to stop it.

As a child, I always had a very special relationship with bees. At my special spot by the river was one huge, fallen cottonwood tree next to where I would camp. Inside this tree's old, hollowed trunk was a swarming hive of activity—the log was home to a beautiful colony of honey bees. I was never afraid to be close to the hive. I would sit just a few feet away and watch them for hours, coming and going, busy at work. I would get totally absorbed in the life and beingness of the bee. I didn't know what meditation or contemplation was, but now I can see that watching the bees was a kind of meditation for me. I forgot myself, my life, my surroundings. I could recognize individual bees, and I think they grew familiar with me, too.

I figured out that if I stilled myself and shut off my mind, and just became one of them, really stepping into their rhythm, they would allow me to share a bit of their honey. I would usually sing a little song to them. I would tell them how beautiful they were, how much I loved them, and how much I wanted to taste their sweet honey, how I promised to take only a little bit. Slowly and with no fear, I would move my hand into the hive and, very delicately, very gently, remove a small piece of the honeycomb, being very careful not to disturb any of the larvae. I would sit on the tree trunk and eat my little piece of honeycomb, still singing along with them. They would let me do this all season long.

Singing to the bees felt natural to me. To speak to any animal, all you need to do is connect into your heart and feel the emotions you wish to share with them. Animals are not so different from you or me. We humans tend not to notice how we act or feel around them—then we wonder why an animal will bite, growl, attack, or run away. In the case with the bees, I didn't just go sticking my hand into the hive and yank out a chunk of honey mindlessly. Doing so would have gotten me stung! It's about treating animals with respect and love. Almost always, when you take the time to get to know an animal and approach it with love and respect, the animal will not react aggressively but will feel your heart's intent and allow you to get close.

Studying bees has taught me much about devotion and selfless love. Bees will stay at the entrance of their hive, protecting the queen bee and the larvae, no matter what is threatening them. Even though they have the ability to fly away at any time, they will stay until the last bee is dead to protect the queen. The queen lives her whole life giving birth to the larvae, the colony. She doesn't take a break to eat or drink—she doesn't even leave the hive. She stays with her family, dedicating her whole life to them. Not one of the bees does anything for itself. It is always for the colony, for each other. For example, when the worker bees go out exploring to find pollen, once they find it, they do not stay and eat it; rather, they immediately return to the colony and tell the others where it is so that they will all have food. Everything is done for the good of the whole. Imagine if we human beings treated each other in this way and felt our unity of being, our interdependence with and responsibility for each other.

I once had a dream in which I was a bee going from flower to flower. At first, I didn't understand its symbolism, but now I am starting to understand what it meant. Just as the bee spreads pollen from flower to flower and allows life to blossom, we humans can also be like the bee, carrying the pollen of love from person to person, ripening and opening each heart that we encounter. Just as the action of the bees enables the fruit to grow and flowers to blossom, we can help fertilize each heart we meet to fulfill its hidden potential and blossom fully into Love.

A Lesson from Badger: Never Take without Asking

Sometimes the lessons you learn from animals are not easy ones. I mentioned in the earlier chapter "Speaking with the Animals" that sometimes an animal shares its medicine with you through an unpleasant interaction such as being bitten or attacked. This counteracts our normal way of thinking about what it means to have an animal totem, but it is often the case. We sometimes get initiated by a certain animal who has something to teach us to help us grow or a gift of strength or character to impart on us. For example, I have been bitten by a rattlesnake, pierced by an owl's claw, and kicked by a horse—all serving a significant purpose. Yet no lesson was as memorable and intense as the one I learned from badger. To this day, I rate any illness that is painful in terms of how it compares to badger. It was an initiation I will never forget.

In the first year that I became Little Grandmother, I had to learn much in a short period of time and sometimes felt like I was on my own. I had been sent various medicine shields, staves, rattles, and sacred medicine tools from indigenous people of several tribes. Some were quite old, and some had been made specifically for me. All these sacred medicine tools made use of animal medicine—fur, claws, feathers, bones. Some of these were from my specific animal protector totems. I was just learning how to understand and use animal medicine in this sacred and ceremonial way. I had much to learn because, one day, I made a great mistake that almost killed me.

I had been on a weekend family trip to Colorado Springs with my children and husband at the time. We were driving on a somewhat rural road in the early evening, when I spotted what I knew to be a badger on the road. We stopped, and I got out to examine it. Unfortunately, it had been dead for several hours. I suddenly remembered a particular medicine staff that I had been given. Knowing that badger medicine is quite powerful, I had the idea to use a badger claw on this staff, to bring badger medicine to my sacred healing work. I thought to myself, "Mother Earth must be giving me a badger claw to use," because it is quite rare to find a dead badger on the road, and this one was clearly in my path. So using my special knife, I removed a claw from the badger and sealed it in a plastic bag to bring home with me.

I am not exaggerating when I say that within fifteen minutes, I grew terribly ill. All of a sudden, I developed a pounding migraine like I have never had before, and my body began convulsing with intense pains. I started to throw up from the pain, and my nose began to bleed. I had a high fever that came on out of nowhere. It was as if I totally lost control of my body. My children were scared because one second, I was completely fine, and the next, I was unable to control my vomiting and convulsing and thought I would pass out. We somehow found a hospital, and I went straight to the emergency room. At the hospital, they ran every kind of test on me—and found nothing. They could see that all my nerves were firing at once and that my brain was inflamed—but they could not tell why. I worried that I was having an aneurism or that I had a brain tumor. They did all kinds of scans on me and gave me whatever they could to help stop the pain and prevent me from vomiting and convulsing every few minutes.

By the next morning, I was feeling a bit better but was still in bad shape. They released me from the hospital as they were unable to find anything physically wrong. I still had aches and pains and a massive migraine that no painkiller could completely quell. When we got home, I went straight to bed and lay there barely moving or opening my eyes for the next twenty-four hours. I really thought I must be dying. While in a semiconscious state, going in and out of fever, I started having visions. I saw me taking the badger claw. I knew all of a sudden that this mysterious illness was related to the badger. I knew it with every ounce of my being. My remorse and regret were unfathomable. I was sweating and felt like I was burning up, but I was also cold and having chills. The high fever lasted several hours.

Finally, around midnight that night, three Native American elders appeared before me in a vision, looking very solemn. Only one of them spoke to me. His voice was low and very calm. He explained to me how all animals are sacred and carry sacred medicines and teachings with them. If we human beings wish to use these medicines, we must ask for them, be worthy of using them, and show deep appreciation and respect for the medicine. Prayers must be offered, and we must be granted permission to use them. I was then shown a vision of myself bending over and taking the badger claw without permission or prayers. They told me that I had to go through this purification to learn and understand. I must remember "never to take without asking." After this purification, badger spirit would be with me—but I should never forget that I was working with a real spirit with a very real power. The spirits must be respected and approached in the most sacred way. When the Native American elders vanished, my fever broke, and my headache finally subsided.

I would never forget after this. I learned the true power of badger and of all animal spirits that night. This experience taught me that even if an animal is dead, you must always ask for permission to use any part of its body and approach it with the utmost respect. You must be thankful for the gift it is giving and for its life and spirit. This was one of my early tests and initiations; I hoped it wouldn't always be such a severe learning curve. Afterward, when I reflected on the incident, I thought it strange that I hadn't offered prayers before taking the badger claw. I was in the habit of asking permission of animals before interacting with them or approaching them, yet I was somehow thrown off guard by the fact that this animal was already dead and the seeming synchronicity of its placement. In my momentary distraction, I was thinking and forgot to feel what needed to happen.

A good rule of thumb for interacting with all of nature is never to take without asking. And never use or take anything without offering your heartfelt gratitude. Although Mother Earth provides everything we need to live and thrive in abundance, she is powerful and deserves our utmost respect and love for the constant gifts she gives us. The more conscious we humans become of our place among countless creatures and living spirits in a living world, the more we pay attention to the little things—how we interact, what we notice—and what we can offer in return.

All Things Are Born of Love

How many of us find ourselves in our day-to-day lives never really seeing the beauty of nature all around us? More often than not, we go about our days driving down the same road to work, passing the same old trees, or looking out of the same old window every day, not really seeing what is happening in nature. Think for a moment about what is outside your kitchen window. What plants do you see day in and day out? Have you ever really looked at them, noticed them, or spoken to them? My prayer is that once we establish a real relationship with nature, we will see these same old trees and plants as the exquisite creations that they are, no longer taking for granted the beauty Mother Earth gives us each day.

Growing up in a Mormon community, I was always taught to pray to Heavenly Father, to give thanks to him and say my prayers to him every night. There was never mention of Mother in Mormonism, and being part of a religion that lacked any Mother bothered me. When I started to become older, I began looking into other religions for evidence of Mother or the feminine. To my great sadness, I found that the feminine was often nowhere to be found in a positive way in other religious texts or teachings.

It was very confusing. On one hand, I was being taught to obey this particular religion as the Word of God, and on the other hand, I was being taught by nature, Mother Earth herself, in a very nurturing and loving way. I was being pulled in two very different directions. Although I believed the Church and tried to uphold the rules to be worthy of God and heaven, having known nothing else, I knew without question that what I was being taught by the voices in nature was just as real. It was a difficult time in my life, trying to find my way, to make sense of life and figure out what path to take and what was truth. When I reached the age of twenty-three, I could no longer stomach what I was being taught by the patriarchal Mormon religion and finally stepped fully into my Mother's arms, never looking back.

When you begin to have a real relationship with Mother Earth, you can experience a bounty of endless love. For me, *Mother* conjures up every emotion there is. She is love and life itself. To remove Mother from religion or from our conception of Creation is to deny the very essence of tenderness, compassion, beauty, and nurturance that is life itself. It is imperative that we have a real relationship with our most essential mother, Mother Earth. To do this, we must first know and understand her. When you start to really know Mother Earth, miracles seem to be everywhere; beauty is bountiful, and your heart is moved to tears at the glimpse of a butterfly or something as simple as a blade of grass. That same old tree or little plant outside your window becomes a real friend, an expression of love for you from your Mother Earth.

Mother Earth is a divine being who gives us our lives, our breath, our food, our water, the magnificent gift of a body. Yet many of us never really look at her. We have become blind to the gifts she gives us each day, and now she is calling out to us to remember that she is alive. She is suffering from a lack of attention and love from her own children. The problem is, if we do not know our Mother, how can we love her?

When we wake up and really pay attention to her, we see that the birds are singing, calling to one another in the most pure and beautiful way, creating love and greater life through their song. We see that the sun is rising once again to grace its beloved, the Earth, with its tender warmth to bring life to the plants and animals.

I remember once lying in my great grandma's apple tree, looking up into the branches. I watched the sun and the wind caressing the leaves as they swayed back and forth, back and forth. It dawned on me that they were dancing, that all life is a dance, a caress. I realized that it is actually love that creates all life on Earth. When you think about how human beings create a life, it is no coincidence that we create new life through the act of love. It is this way throughout the whole creation: the wind blows and caresses the pollen from a flower, or a pine cone is blown from the top of a tree, and in this loving gesture, life is born. The pollen then finds another flower or plant with which to mingle, and it creates life. The pine cone that was birthed through the dance between the wind and the tree falls to the Earth, and then one day it happens: beautiful raindrops fall, and the rain mixes with the soil. Through this act of communion and love, the seed sprouts into life. Nature is perfect in its balance, rhythm, and knowing.

A natural fire can sweep through the forest, in its passion burning the old and dead parts away and leaving the raw and exposed Earth open to new sparks of life. Something we see as destructive is really a passionate birth of life. In the very peak of the fire, the heat rises to the exact temperature that a sealed pine cone needs to melt its resin and loosen and release its seeds. All things in nature are in a dance of giving and receiving. All things are alive in love and given to us out of love. Even the fruits and vegetables that we eat were not only born in an act of love but have grown in a perfect way to help the human body, to nourish and strengthen us.

When you understand the give-and-take, the essence of love that has created all the life around you, you can more deeply appreciate the apple you will eat for lunch or even the piece of toast that started out as grain. That little plant outside your window has been there all along growing and trying to be as beautiful as it can be—for *you*. When you start to truly know Mother Earth and the beautiful acts of love she is constantly giving you, then you can really love her. You can have a real relationship with her. Life truly begins. You see the love that is transpiring and the life that is being created in every act of nature. You take the time to say thank you to the things you eat and to the plants around you. Just as you were conceived in the act of love, so has everything else been made in the energy of love, born of the Mother's tenderness, generosity, and beauty.

The Divine Order in Creation

Mother Earth is a spectacular source of life, governed by the ultimate wisdom of the Creator, from the smallest seed that knows just when to burst into life to the largest whale that knows to migrate north for food. All things are made by an ultimate source of intelligence, and in every speck of life, we can see this magical intelligence. There is much untapped knowledge within nature. We might find answers for many problems in the world, from architectural breakthroughs to cures for diseases, if we were to look deeply enough.

How is it that the bees instinctively know where to find food and how to tell each other where to find this food or that the cicadas hibernate deep within the Earth for seventeen years before hatching all at once and crawling up the tree trunks? Every blade of grass grows with a great purpose. Every animal is a pivotal part of the circle of life. We, too, are part of this wise circle of life, this vast storehouse of knowledge hidden in creation, in nature. We intuitively want to know as much as we can, to live up to our fullest potential, to unlock the mystery of life. Just as the red crabs are called to rush to the beach to lay their eggs at a pivotal part of the moon's cycle or the sand hill cranes are called to migrate across the western plains, we, too, are called to become our truest, highest selves.

We are a real part of the great mystery of nature that is integrated into the highest plan of life. All things on this wondrous planet are engaged in a miraculous dance of life, of birth, growth, and death. Just as certain trees or flowers wait their whole lives to bloom at just the right moment, so has humanity waited for its pivotal time to bloom, to burst into full awareness. That time is now. Something is calling us to burst into our fullest potential, to awaken and bloom into our most beautiful intelligence. We are so much more than we have been led to believe. We are great sparks of the divine source of life, and it is time for us now to step fully into that being. We can set down at last our urge to feel like victims weighed down by life's struggles. We can fully know that we are the ultimate creations of Great Spirit and that within us lay the vast intelligence of Love.

We can be the creators of our own experience, if we will just remember how miraculous we really are. It is time to see our beautiful Mother Earth for the splendid miracle she really is and that all things are born in love, for a purpose in the mysterious circle of life. We are the creators of our lives. We are in charge of calling forth what we want to experience. Through our intention and through our feelings, emotions, and dreams, we pull into our experience what we want to live. Just as the pull of the moon's gravity causes the great waves on our planet, our higher selves are calling to us, urging us to step fully into our creative power and be the wondrous and magical beings that we can be.

Just as every piece of fruit and every vegetable is grown in divine order to provide nourishment and life, so have our higher selves been created to provide us with limitless energy, love, and light to feed and nourish our bodies and spirits. Until we start to see Mother Earth as the blessed divine being she is in all her wondrous and magical intelligence, we will never see this within ourselves. We are our Mother's children; we are part of her creation, part of her beauty and her unfathomable wisdom. When we start to realize this, we start to realize just how amazing we really are. We human beings are a part of something so vastly amazing and perfect that it is hard to fathom. It is time for us to start loving ourselves for the incredible creations we are and to start loving our Mother, who gives us this opportunity to live within her boundless dance of life.

PART II
Remember Who You Are

Return of the Ancestors

In April 2009, I was privileged to be able to lead one of the most powerful ceremonies I have ever experienced. The ceremony of which I speak, held just north of Santa Fe in the high desert of New Mexico, supported the official Return of the Ancestors International Gathering, which took place in Arizona between April 18 and 28, 2009. The gathering in Arizona brought together indigenous elders, spiritual leaders, shamans, wisdom keepers, and people of all kinds, both indigenous and nonindigenous, from all over the planet for days of ceremony, meetings, and healing rituals. The period in April chosen for the ceremony actually corresponded with Mayan and Hopi prophesies about what would happen during this time period.

It was to be a time when the healing of Mother Earth would begin, a time when the heavens would open, pouring down energies of assistance, light, and love to help us as human beings remember who we are. In doing so, we would be able to rise to a higher consciousness. It would herald a time of the return of ancient wisdom and ways of being about which we had forgotten, a turning point for humanity. The Mayan grand elder Don Alejandro Cirilo Perez Oxlaj, "the keeper of all Mayan teachings," had spoken of how at this time, we were being offered a crucial question to decide. Were we, as human beings, capable of change? Our answer was crucial to the future of the planet. It was time for us to remember how to live in harmony with all of life again, to respect and listen to Mother Earth, to respect the feminine and understand the need for balance between her and the masculine on the planet. Our ancestors lived this way, and yet their ways and wisdom have long been forgotten. It was time to invite our ancestors' wisdom and ancient ways of being back into our lives. It was time to offer all the love in our hearts to heal those who had come before and who now were waiting to return and guide us at this time of great transformation.

I had been contacted in December 2008 by those who were coordinating the gathering in Arizona and working with the Continental Council of Indigenous Elders under the leadership of Don Alejandro Oxlaj. I was asked to hold ceremony for the New Mexico and Colorado region because the Arizona gathering was already full and so many people wanted to participate. There would be gatherings held in various places all over the world during this time period, linked with the massive international gathering in Arizona.

This would be my first public ceremony. Frankly, I was terrified. Yet I knew how globally important this was and sensed that it would be a further initiation for me, bringing me even closer to my true purpose. Even though I knew nothing about how to put together a several-day-long event, or even how to get people to come, I decided to take a leap of faith and do it. I told some friends and associates about the ceremony, and they helped spread the word. Those who heard about it were excited and eager to participate. Soon things were set in motion. People stepped forward to help at every turn, and a core group of about fifteen people who felt called to support the ceremony in a direct way began regularly gathering to organize. I am so grateful to this core group—my "council"—who were instrumental in making this profound event happen! We had no idea how large or small the gathering would be and did not directly advertise it. Yet word spread by word of mouth and cyberspace. We figured that whoever was meant to be there would be there, and regardless of how many people came, we would do what we were called to do.

On an inner level, I began praying for guidance on what I would need to do and how we could support and participate in the energies that would be available during this powerful time. So in the months preceding, I began to receive specific guidance from Spirit on the key ceremonies that needed to be conducted. I learned that other shamans and wisdom keepers who were leading ceremonies in other parts of the world were receiving the same guidance. The ceremony would be held from April 18 to 20 on private land just north of Santa Fe, in an area called "Rio en Medio." This spot was flat and open, bordered by a nearby natural stream and surrounded by stretching views of the Sangre de Cristo Mountains. The owner of the land, a friend named Lars, had offered this lovely spot and specially prepared the land with devotion and care for the sacred ceremony that would occur there. I knew that each day would have a particular focus, and a particular ceremony would need to be conducted. These three days would focus on healing Mother Earth, healing the masculine and feminine, and sharing certain prophecies and information that had been coming through to wisdom keepers all over the planet.

To Become a Hollow Bone

Though I had a sense of the key ceremonies that would need to take place, I knew I would have to trust Spirit to guide me in the moment. Each day would begin early and end at about five o'clock in the evening. I truly did not know what to expect, what to say, or what to do. Even a few days before the ceremony, I still had a very foggy idea of how things would flow and what might happen when. But I knew that my real job was to be open to Spirit, to be a hollow bone and listen to guidance from the ancestors themselves about what to say and do. The day before the ceremony, I remember being out in the yard among the pinions and junipers, in a special spot where I would often go to pray. When I finished praying and was walking back toward the house, I saw something I will never forget because it gave me a feeling of exhilaration and a certainty that all would be okay. Everything would happen as it was supposed to.

The land in front of me and all around me suddenly appeared like a desert. I saw people, thousands of people, in the hills and stretching as far as the eye could see. They were walking toward me. They were of many races and cultures, and based on their dress, they appeared to be from different time periods. The older people were in the front, followed by men, women, and children. One particular man was naked, except for what looked like a jaguar or leopard pelt across his shoulder. Some of the elders were incredibly regal and had a spiritual dignity about them. This was a sea of people, and they were coming for the ceremony. I had never seen anything like it. These were the ancestors, and they were coming. They were coming to witness!

When I walked into the house, tears were streaming down my face from the beauty of the vision. I knew then that despite my worries and anxiety, this ceremony was not about me. I was not in charge of making anything happen. Something much bigger was happening here. We were not in charge of what would occur—Spirit was. The other side would help direct this ceremony. I would merely need to listen and to be open to Spirit. My relief was immense. Though I was still a bit nervous about having to lead the ceremony and hold the sacred space, I had a deep, inward sense that everything would work out the way it was supposed to—and that something beautiful would occur.

Day 1: Healing of Sacred Mother Earth

On the first day of ceremony, Friday, April 18, 2009, about twenty hardy souls gathered before sunrise at the ceremonial site. It was a cold, snowy morning, and clouds covered the rolling foothills. It had snowed the night before, and flakes were coming down intermittently even then. We were all bundled up in blankets and coats, clutching thermoses of hot tea and taking turns warming our frozen toes by the fire.

This first day was devoted to healing our sacred Mother Earth. In near darkness, we created the large, sacred circle, a medicine wheel of stones, then we made an altar in the center of the circle. As the sun rose, we began prayers, and an elder who had studied with the Hopi for many years played the flute and led us in a beautiful song. One of the most important aspects of this day would be focusing our healing energies, love, and gratitude to help heal Mother Earth. Specifically, we would send our healing prayers into a special crystal that would be placed in Mother Earth. We would be using this crystal to send our love into Mother Earth and to connect with and strengthen the ancient ley lines of energy that connected this spot to other hot spots around the planet. This would, in turn, strengthen Mother Earth's energy grid and help raise the energetic frequency on the planet.

As we set the large, cylindrical quartz crystal upright, half-buried in the Earth in the center of the circle, and began sending all our loving, healing energies into it, something unusual started to happen. I began to see *them* again. Just as I had the day before, I started to see, all around us and stretching into the far hills, a sea of people. They were of all tribes and colors and nationalities. My joy was so full that it felt as though my heart would burst. I could not keep my tears from flowing as I told everyone what I was seeing. Even today, I get goose bumps and I swell with love and gratitude when I think of that morning. What was even more amazing to me was that I could see energy pouring down from the heavens to Earth in bands or pillars of light.

I had begun seeing these tubelike pillars of energy coming down from the sky here and there. I had seen these pillars of light grow in size, but on this first day of ceremony, it seemed to me that the heavens opened and these streams of light grew wider and expanded, merging with each other until they became one large pillar cascading down from the sky to Earth. Many people in the circle felt something happening, and there was a collective intake of breath at the moment the pillars became one. The massive amount of energy flowing from the heavens to Earth that day was undeniable.

Day 2: Healing the Masculine and Feminine

The second day of ceremony was, and I think I speak for everyone who attended, the most profound and powerful for all of us. This day was extremely difficult but crucial to the purpose and fulfillment of the gathering. The second day of ceremony was dedicated to the healing of the masculine and the feminine. Through dreams, visions, and lessons, I learned what this day was going to be about and how to perform what was needed. The more I learned, the more I became wary of this day.

I found myself in tears the night before, and sick to my stomach. I struggled with my conflicted feelings. I knew I still held much rage and grief from being sexually and physically abused as a child. Could I hold the space for what needed to happen? Was I willing to go into my own wounded self and release the pain I had suffered? Was I healed enough myself to be able to do this ceremony? All I could do was pray for help and surrender.

The reason for this particular ceremony was to acknowledge our deep wounds in the area of sexuality and gender. We cannot heal the Earth until we heal ourselves, and the deepest wounds we carry as human beings are those buried deep within our masculine and feminine psyches. These two energies have been so out of balance for so long in human civilization that it is impossible not to see the damage created by this imbalance in almost every living human on the globe. It is so great an imbalance, in fact, that without rebalancing and healing, we human beings simply will not be able to survive, and nor will our planet. The feminine needs to be healed and awakened on the planet so that the great wisdom of love, tenderness, compassion, beauty, and receptivity can restore a healthful way of being on Earth and with each other. The wisdom of the Mother and of Mother Earth needs to lead us back to wholeness. Yet the masculine would need to be healed, as well, and brought back into harmony and balance from out of the destructive grip of control, force, ego, and will—back into the heart, where it might serve and protect all life.

I began talking to the group about the great imbalance. I shared how the collective negative masculine energies have created a massive wound on our planet through thousands of years of domination, rape, torture, warfare, molestation, violence, and horrific acts toward children, women, and men. Both men and women bear the wounds of this loss of heart, this trauma and the alienation it causes.

Most of the men in the circle had no idea what was about to happen, and it was probably just as well, because some of them would have wanted to exit then and there. Spirit had shown me the exact formations the men and women were to be in for these ceremonies and what needed to be done. I did not envy the men in the circle as I asked them to stand and join hands. My heart wept for them deeply as I instructed them on what needed to be done and what was being asked of them. They were to go inward as deeply as they could, to witness all these atrocities, to witness the grief and pain of the feminine, to feel and release these negative energies, not just for their own lives, but for those lives that had come before them throughout history. As I spoke, my whole body shuddered as the gut-wrenching sorrow and pain started to build inside me, as I asked these good-hearted men to do such a hard thing. I must say now that the men in the circle were some of the strongest and purest hearts I have ever met. I assured them that I did not place any blame on them as individuals, and I swore to keep them safe and grounded to Mother Earth and Father Sky the entire time. I asked all the women to gather in a larger circle around them to hold space and send them loving light and energy as they endured their ordeal.

I weep when I remember what transpired in the circle. As we began and the men held hands in a circle, their tears began to fall. Even the women who stood in a circle around the men, some of whom were their husbands and partners, were weeping. I have a hard time finding the words to describe the suffering these beautiful men went through. Their anguish, their cries, were so deep and raw. Some of the men coughed an agonizing cough to rid them of thoughts and images. Some men tried to fight off vomiting; others wept and convulsed, overcome with grief. I stayed as grounded as I could as I went from man to man, raising my energies as high as I could to hold them in a safe and held space, grounding them to Mother Earth and Father Sky, as I was instructed to by my guides, so that the pain and suffering could be given away through their feet and heads. The women who encircled the men started humming and singing as one voice, sending loving sounds to the men to help them stay grounded and in the heart. One man collapsed, having a kind of cathartic fit. I became alarmed, and I realized that I could no longer hold the space alone and asked the energy healers and Reiki masters present to step in and put their hands on the men to help them. I watched and listened, praying for it to be over, to get some guidance that we could stop, as the pain of the men was almost unbearable for us all.

All the while, I not only watched the men closely but witnessed the male ancestors who were there, gathered behind us in a sea of people, move forward and step into the men one at a time, then exit. As this would happen, the men's cries would change as they expressed the suffering and pain of the different spirits who took part. Then, finally, I heard a calm but strong voice say, "It is done!" I quickly announced that we had accomplished what was asked of us and had all of the women go to the men, hold them, thank them, and love them. We all wept together, completely drained. We held on to one another in a tight embrace. I had known this day would be hard, but not even I knew how extremely powerful and life changing this ceremony would be for us and, quite possibly, our planet.

We all took a long break before the feminine healing would began. This time, I was instructed to have the women form a semicircle, like a chalice or a womb. The men were to stand in a straight line across this semicircle, sealing off the two corners of the chalice. Again, we all held hands as I instructed the women to go deep within and let all the abuse, all the grief and rage, the experience of the feminine throughout millennia, rise to the surface. I was fully expecting the healing of the feminine ceremony to be much worse, harder than the masculine, but it was different. It began with quiet sobs as the women thought of their own abuse, their children's abuse, their mothers' and grandmothers' and great grandmothers' lives and what they had lived as women. It was a low sobbing, a quiet weeping that went on for a long time. Then I was instructed to place my hands on their lower bellies. I have to admit that I didn't understand my instructions at first. As I went from one individual to the next, I started to see what was happening. The women were still holding on to their buried pain, suppressing it, as we have all been taught to do. It was a survival tactic, and we had learned it well. But as I went from womb to womb, the screams and cries broke out. Things started to surface in a huge wave of sorrow. All the women fell to the ground. Some lay on their bellies, some on their backs; many were in the fetal position as they wept, wailed, and cried out for all the abuse and injustice, neglect, disrespect, domination, and oppression women have suffered.

Just as in the men's ceremony, I witnessed the ancient ones' spirits step into some of the women and then leave. They took their turns being witnessed through the different women lying on the ground. I witnessed one woman turn into a bright, almost metallic light, and after the ceremony, I discovered that several others had witnessed the same thing. The men stood around the women in the protective chalice shape, witnessing, sending love and support to them as they grieved. Soon the answer came: "It is done!" and with that, I had the men step in and hold the women, thank them, and give them their love. The men held the women tenderly for quite some time before we brought the ceremony to a close. We were all emotionally drained but elated, as well. It was as if each one of us had helped to lighten the load of the world's grief, which had been buried in us like a huge weight on the collective human heart.

Something monumental had been released. We had grieved not just for ourselves but for generations of our ancestors, men and women who had been deeply wounded. We had cleared more space in the human heart for love by acknowledging and witnessing the wounds of men and women, of the masculine and feminine. I had been worried about whether I could hold the space, but this ceremony turned out to be the greatest gift to me and the greatest learning and healing I had experienced up until that point. I could let go of some of my judgment and fear of the masculine I had been carrying since childhood. I had now seen loving men wholeheartedly grieve for the wrongdoings against the feminine and could feel their own pain at having to carry it and what they had suffered in being men.

I felt a real love for the men present and knew them as my brothers. I knew that there were many beautiful, loving men on the planet and that many men, too, had been victimized by the imbalanced masculine. I knew that we were in this together and that both masculine and feminine had essential roles to play in the beautiful new Earth we were helping to bring into being. I received a healing I never expected from this day and am deeply grateful to the men and women who participated. It helped me on my journey toward healing from years of abuse and from the rage and grief I had always carried for what had been done to me and what has been done to women and children historically. For the first time in my life, I could feel a much deeper compassion and love for men. I knew that change was possible, that we could and would heal and change things.

Day 3: A Sharing of Wisdom and Prophecies

The third day was dedicated to the wisdom keepers' teachings, the lessons I had been receiving since a child and some of the prophesies that I had been given from the other side to share. This day was much more lighthearted than the first two. I spoke about the times to come and how we, as children of our Mother Earth, needed to remember the Great I AM that we each are and how to live from the heart, not the mind. This day marked the momentous symbolic event of the Condor of the South and the Eagle of the North finally flying wingtip to wingtip, a prophesy that has been spoken about by indigenous peoples for thousands of years. This was the time in which humanity would remember that the heart is the connection to the Great I AM that sent us here.

On this last day, I shared information that other wisdom keepers and I had been receiving about changes to come on planet Earth. Some of this information had to do with the star beings who have always been here and who will once again very soon be revealed to be our cosmic family, unimaginably changing the way we human beings see reality and our place in the cosmos. It is known that these star people came to our planet before known human civilization and hid buried truths and teachings that would be rediscovered and used again when human beings were able to comprehend them spiritually. The Return of the Ancestors gathering and affiliated global ceremonies marked the start of the period of rapid human spiritual evolution, when all these things would come to pass and be revealed.

For me personally, the third day marked the start of something profound and unforeseen. The ceremony in Santa Fe was a deeply profound experience and huge learning for me. I learned that I could walk into something daunting and scary with complete trust that Spirit would guide and direct me. I realized that if I could listen and trust, the help would come, and that these sacred ceremonies were in actuality being performed by the other side—not just by us! It was false thinking that I was in any way running the show. I felt such gratitude afterward and knew that Spirit was with us all those days.

I did not realize at the time, however, how much this one ceremony would change my life. It was the description of this ceremony via YouTube videos that touched so many people's hearts and inspired them to want to love and heal themselves and Mother Earth. It was not long after this event in April 2009 that I began receiving invitations to visit faraway lands, to work with larger groups of people, and to speak publicly. Once again, I had to face my fear of failure and my lack of preparation; once again, I would have to trust in Spirit. I was never prepared to be a public speaker, and to this day, if I did not give over to Spirit my trust that this is what I'm supposed to do, and that *something* will take over, I could never do it without falling to pieces!

In fact, when I first started speaking internationally, I fainted on stage in front of several hundred people in Denmark. I had been jet-lagged and somewhat overwhelmed and started to feel myself fading out during my talk. The next thing I knew, I was on the floor in the back surrounded by about ten people, who were all working on me energetically. That was a little more drama than anyone had bargained for. Luckily, such a thing never happened again, and I learned better how to ground and energetically prepare myself for public events. But speaking is still not an easy thing for me to do. Spirit works in mysterious ways and must really want this message shared; otherwise, I would surely be hiding out in the forest and speaking with the birds, looking under rocks and scouting out the creatures in safe anonymity, as I had done for the first thirty years of my life.

The Shift from Mind to Heart

There are two great ancient civilizations that today hold the keys to living from the heart: the Mayans and the aboriginal people. They still live from the heart, and they are the ones who are teaching us now to live from the heart again. For thousands of years, human civilization has developed in a particular way. We have developed the capacity of our rational minds to the extent that we have made great inventions and built great cities, and in very recent years, we have made a huge leap in our discovery of new technologies. There is no doubt that we have done some amazing things. But the problem is that we have left the heart behind. We stopped acting from and making decisions from the heart and feeling our connectedness to all life. We have overvalued the rational, logical mind and believe only in what we can see and experience with our bodily senses. This was never how it was intended to be. We are being asked now to start living from the heart again, and this is one of the messages I have been asked specifically to share.

This is the universal law: *the more loving you are, the more intelligent you become.* Just imagine all the advancements in technology we have created with our minds in just the last ten years. It's mind-boggling. Yet we still cannot solve some of the most urgent problems facing us today. The greatest problem is how to heal what we have done to the Earth already and how to stop doing what we have been doing to her ever since human beings forgot their connection to the web of life. If we have been able to create so much using just our minds, imagine what we might create if we were operating from the heart! Mind would not be inactive or unused—it would grow much more powerful because it would be in right relationship to heart, to the source of being and to creation. If we stop operating from an ego-driven mental consciousness, we will stop striving for meaningless things that gratify only the smallest part of who we are. We will stop wasting our mental energy and will start directing every ounce of our hearts and minds to healing the Earth and creating bounty for all beings. We could create a paradise on Earth unlike anything we have seen before.

I have been taught by Spirit that Mother Earth is sacred and that human beings will not be allowed to kill her. She is sacred to all life-forms in the universe, not just to human beings. We need to raise our vibration high enough so that we can shift with her into a higher state of being. We have been causing her great harm for so long that something major must happen to correct the path we are treading, to help her breathe again. For human beings, the situation is urgent. We must shift into a higher consciousness if we are to remain on planet Earth as her children.

If you listen, none of the indigenous elders or wisdom keepers on our planet are saying, "Now you must go and do something"; rather, they are saying, "Be." They are telling us to *be the change*, to focus on being rather than on doing, for once. If enough of us can connect with our hearts and the Love that is there, the Love that is all around us in nature, and understand the beauty and sacredness of this life we are given, we will flip the ruling consciousness of the planet from mind to heart.

Flipping the Bobber of Global Consciousness

One of the ways in which I receive spiritual messages and information is through what seems like a large TV screen that opens in my field of vision. In this way, I can also communicate with other wisdom keepers and beings elsewhere on the planet. I call it my "picture show." Once I was shown a specific lesson about how this change from mind to heart consciousness will happen. I saw a bobber floating on the water, just like when you go fishing. If you catch a fish, it bobs down under the water. One half is red, and the other half is white. The bobber represented planetary consciousness. I saw that right now on planet Earth, the white side of the bobber is showing and the red is submerged. The white represents mind consciousness—how humanity is obsessed with thinking, judging, and perceiving reality from this narrow place. The red side represents heart consciousness, living from the reality of love—a much larger consciousness that makes us aware that we are all brothers and sisters and that we can create our own reality. Though the white side was on top, I was shown that the bobber was starting to flip. There are thousands of people on the planet right now who are extremely committed to changing the consciousness on the planet, who are very dedicatedly working for this. More and more people are waking up every day, realizing that we each have a divine spark within us, that who we are is much larger than we ever imagined.

The more of us who change our own consciousness and wake up to who we are, the more we will help that bobber flip over to heart consciousness. It isn't required that everyone on the planet make the leap because love vibration is the highest vibration in existence—it is more powerful than mind or ego consciousness. If enough people wake up and start living from the heart, we will change the ruling consciousness on the planet. We have the ability to flip the bobber, to change the ruling consciousness on planet Earth. In fact, it is only a matter of time—I believe that we will do it very soon. And when it does flip, everything will change.

Our world will change. We will collectively understand that we can create the kind of life we want on Earth with each other, that whatever we can dream, we can create. This is when we will begin to create a paradise on Earth and to find solutions to our most urgent problems—to clean up what we have done to Mother Earth and create a more balanced, just, and beautiful human society. The way we see reality, the way we see each other, the way we view what we are capable of and incapable of—it will all change. We will realize, all of a sudden, that we can create reality as we wish it to be, that we can do amazing things!

The key is that we must remember that we are gods and goddesses, not the limited beings we think we are. We are sparks of the divine consciousness. Each of us has a Great I AM that sent a spark of us here to experience and learn from being in a human body and from having this amazing human heart.

By living from love and being in the heart, we will remember that most sacred truth that we are all brothers and sisters and children of one mother—Mother Earth. We are not separate from each other or from any other life-form. What happens to one of us happens to all of us. Because human energy is identical to Earth energy, what happens to Mother Earth also happens to us, and vice versa. Yet we are capable of changing this world in which we live. Spirit has shown me that at the time of the great shifting of Earth, humanity will unify as one family, one tribe, and that this tribe will be a rainbow tribe, one made of many colors. The only way this tribe can come together is through realizing that we are one heart, not actually separate from each other. What one person or people feel, we all feel. When one person or part of creation is unhealthy, we are all going to be unhealthy. It affects us all. Though our ecological systems have been showing us this interdependency for many centuries, we are only now starting to understand it. We are not separate from each other or from Mother Earth. We are here to learn, to love, and to create—we are here to love each other and all life. Planet Earth is the planet of the heart, the heart chakra of the cosmos. It is our ability to love and feel emotion that is our greatest gift and that makes us so interesting to the other beings of the cosmos (and there are many!).

Each day, we can let our hearts be broken open by the beauty of creation, by the beauty of this experience. We can take the time each day to feel gratitude to Mother Earth, to Great Spirit, for all that we are and have. We can start to let go of those beliefs and ideas that do not serve our lives individually or collectively any longer. We are not what we do for a living or how much money we have; we are not what others think of us or even what we think of ourselves; we are not our identities, our status, our accumulated experiences, our successes and mistakes, or our personalities. We must let go of all that we've been told we should want and of what we've been told matters and decide these things for ourselves from our deepest hearts. What matters most? What brings you true joy? Who are you? What would you live for, if you had the courage to? What brings you tears of gratitude and wonder? When do you feel most at home in yourself? To delve into these questions is the first step toward touching what it feels like to live in the heart.

How Do We Start Living from the Heart?

But how exactly do we start living from the heart? How do we know when we are in the heart? Like so much in life, the answer is quite simple, but because our minds complicate things, it can seem difficult at first. For me, being in the heart has to do with being *present,* not just to my surroundings and what is before me but to myself, to my feelings as they are happening. There are many spiritual teachers and paths describing the same thing, perhaps using different language to do so. But they point to the same state of being, which is really a kind of innocence and openness to life.

Basically, when I speak of living *from the heart*, I mean living from a place of presence in the moment, where the mind isn't ruling the show. I am not thinking about everything as I am experiencing it—I'm feeling it. I'm sensing it, not separating myself from what I am experiencing through my thoughts about it. Using my heart rather than my mind to perceive reality implies a connectedness between everything I see, touch, and sense and my own inner being. When we are living from the heart, we *feel* that we are one with other living things, with everything that is; we feel that what happens to one person is also, on some level, happening to others because we are all alive and made of consciousness and energy. We are not really separate from each other. To our intellects, this seems like a stretch and very different from how we've been taught to see reality. Yet we have all experienced some form of this state of being, even if only for moments at a time.

Sometimes this state is accompanied by a quiet contentment, a feeling of great peace; sometimes it is accompanied by a kind of ecstasy, the sheer bliss of being alive, the bliss of loving life; sometimes it comes with a heightened awareness of suffering, of the pain being experienced, right now, by other beings on the planet, or of the great mystery of existence, which includes both bliss and agony and everything in between, in each moment. We feel more—and are willing to feel all that this sometimes crazy existence offers us. We let ourselves be *opened* by life. We make ourselves more receptive to others, to each day, to each moment.

We all do this naturally in our own way, even without thinking about it too much. Chances are you have a way of tuning yourself to your own heart, a way of coming home to yourself. For me, interacting with the natural world is a surefire way of bringing me back into my heart, into a deeper presence. To really interact with an animal, I must use my perception and senses in a different way than we are taught to; I must trust my senses and instincts. I must open myself to the reality in which animals live, which is utterly in the moment, in harmony with Mother Earth. One cannot communicate with an animal if one is caught up in ego and mind. One must become totally pure of heart and learn to truly listen.

What tunes you to your own deepest heart? For some people, being with children or with animals helps bring them into their hearts. For other people, music does it best, shifting consciousness from a feeling of separateness to a feeling of unity and harmony. To know when you are in your heart, follow the emotion. Chances are you will feel greater emotion when you shift into your heart. This may not always be positive emotion such as joy, gratitude, or bliss. If you have spent a long time away from your own heart, you may feel some things you've been trying not to feel. You may feel grief or sadness. You may start to feel whatever you have been holding back. This has to happen so that your heart can be cleansed and healed. You will have to feel what is in your heart to air it out and release whatever sorrows and hurts you are holding. This will create space for even greater Love, even greater beauty, to exist in you. But we have to be willing to get real with ourselves and feel what we are feeling in any moment.

Before I give a talk or workshop, I will sometimes use music to tune myself to my heart. If I've gotten stuck in thinking, or if I feel limited or small as "Kiesha" and want to really connect to my higher self, I will listen to music that stirs my highest emotions. If I can get to that place where I am moved to tears, fully surrendering my consciousness to the music, then I will always find the guidance I need. If I can become the music and get myself out of the way, then I can clear the way for my spirit guides to communicate with me. What actually happens when you do this is that you are tuning in to a higher frequency. If reality is multidimensional, then we exist on many levels simultaneously. There are realms of light and higher Love to which we can tune in. Our higher selves are always accessing these realms, but we need to make space and attune to that vibration. The vibration is always there, but we are simply not choosing to tune in to it most of the time.

When you feel life with your heart and refuse to think away what you are feeling and sensing, or to judge yourself, you will invite your higher self to take charge of your life. We *know* so much that we disregard and refuse to pay attention to. We often sense the right path to take, but because it doesn't make sense to us, or we cannot rationally figure out how A will lead to B, and how B will lead to C, we refuse to listen. We think certain things are impossible and believe in the bill of goods we have been sold as reality. We have much more choice than we realize. If we can start trusting our hearts to guide us, we will live in an utterly different way. We will base our judgments and actions on what love dictates, not on what will be most profitable, easy, or safe. This is what will allow humanity to unify as one heart, one tribe. And when this happens, we will have concern and love for each other, just as we would for our own families, and the world in which we live will change in ways we can only now imagine.

You are the Great I AM

After I became Little Grandmother, I was taught some very particular lessons about what we need to understand and remember to step into our full potential as human beings on planet Earth. One of the first lessons I was taught had to do with understanding the nature of higher self. The term that Spirit used was new to me. Spirit said to me, "Remember that you are the Great I AM." You may use a different language to convey this idea of the higher self and its connection to the All, the divine source, but these are the terms Spirit has directly used with me. In other words, you are a spark of the divine Light and Love that created you. I was shown that each human being is really a divine spark and that we are more akin to gods and goddesses than we think. We have so much more creative and spiritual potential than we realize. If we knew how to access our higher selves and the limitless wisdom that is there, we could create miracles and utterly change how we experience reality on Earth.

The greatest limitation we carry is the false idea that we are flawed, sinful, and imperfect. You are perfect just as you are. Your higher self is divine, and what you experience as yourself is just a small spark of the divinity you really are. This divine spark that is you came to Earth to learn certain things and have certain experiences. This journey you are on is exactly what you needed and wanted to learn. There are no mistakes. Your higher self loves you and is directing you and leading you where you need to go. Each of us is living on a different level or spectrum of human experience, not because we are higher or lower but because that's what we came here for. We're expressing a particular vibration and dimension of being. There is no sense in judging oneself or one's neighbor because we are all on our own journey. The path we are on is perfect for us; we chose it before we came here. Knowing this, how can we judge a person, ourselves or another, for who that person is?

This is not to say that people do not do wrong or make harmful choices. This human experience is all about duality and free will. I have suffered from the poor choices of others, when certain adults in my life abused me as a young person. The choice to hurt another human being is always the wrong choice—that is cosmic law. Yet I have come to realize that those early painful experiences have played an essential role in my journey and in making me who I am today. The effect of everything we experience creates who we are and how we develop. I have learned, through much pain and inner struggle, that sometimes those things that happen to us that seem wholly negative and damaging can also have hidden blessings.

However, it is up to each person to decide how to interpret what happens in his or her life. Personally, I have come to a place where, though I can never condone the abuse that happened, I can see the divinity of the ones who abused me, that they had higher selves, too, and came from the same divine source. I choose to see my abuse as having meaning and a purpose. Yet I would never be able to tell someone who has been victimized, "You must have chosen this," nor would I attempt to tell that person what his or her abuse means—to do so would be callous and uncompassionate. No one standing outside can make that judgment call for another person or say how another should learn from his or her particular experiences. Knowing that there may have been a spiritual purpose in something does not take away the sense of injustice or the rage and pain a person can experience in being a victim. Yet we can begin to consider that perhaps the experience wasn't meaningless from the perspective of the higher self. Perhaps my Great I AM did choose to have the experience of abuse to learn and grow in certain ways. But this is not to say that I chose it. Only from the cosmic perspective of the soul can I imagine there being a larger purpose in children's suffering. My higher self may have chosen it, but I did not. This is an important distinction.

The key to healing is to experience the freedom of knowing that we are much more vast and limitless than we realize and to always move in the direction that serves our highest good, our wholeness. It is crucial to realize that we have a choice in how we relate to our experience and what we do with it. We can let it make us smaller and feel damaged and victimized, or we can use it as an opportunity to become larger than we are, more loving, more compassionate and wise. We can release judgment, as much as possible, and entertain a sense of mystery and wonder about our experience. This only comes from becoming larger than our experience, knowing that we are not these limited selves that we think; we are not just what we experience, or our personalities, or our identities—we are a spark of God, of divine Love and light, and the greater beings we are is untouched by what happens to us here.

If we can resist judging everything so much, it will free up much space for being the loving beings we are. If I am not so busy judging you and your life path, I can love you just as you are. I can love the Great I AM you are, knowing that you are here on a particular journey to learn certain things and experience life through a certain lens. I don't have to change you, and you don't have to change me. I can appreciate the thrilling diversity of expressions of humanity we have on this planet; I can free myself from thinking that I am better and you need to be like me, or that you are better and I need to be like you. These kinds of judgments come from thinking we are not enough as we are. We usually judge people by appearances and make all kinds of assessments about them, forgetting that they are divine sparks, too, and are here to express a certain vibration on the planet—all as part of the great cosmic tapestry of life on planet Earth.

Seeing with the Heart

A while back, when I was in Arkansas to conduct a ceremony, I was taught a lesson in a dream about judgment—how we sometimes truly don't see the forest for the trees. In my dream, I was confronted by a very scary looking man who appeared as a vagrant, with a beard and missing teeth, wild eyes, and dirty clothes. He was beckoning to me. In the dream, I had an immediate distrust of him because he looked homeless. I moved away from him and went over to be with some young people who were dressed nicely and looked like normal people. When I woke, I knew the dream was important and sat down to meditate on it. Spirit told me that the man had had something important to teach me. He had had a message for me, but I had missed out on it because I had turned away. I had judged his appearance and had not seen him with my heart.

Part of the human experience has to do with discrimination, judging things as good or bad, safe or dangerous, wanted or unwanted. Duality is a cornerstone of the human experience. Yet when our hearts are open, we are not as likely to make such automatic judgments. We can see a lot more than the surface mind can see. Many times, a jewel is hidden under an unattractive or threatening appearance. We have to open our hearts to see the reality of a thing, what it really is and not what it seems to be. We could learn so much if we were to open ourselves to things instead of automatically closing. It can be a hard call, especially when we judge something as threatening or dangerous. But the problem is that we use only our minds and our eyes to decide, not our hearts. In the dream, I could have stopped to feel the man with my heart, to take the time to find out who he was, to talk to him. Often, taking such a risk is worth it. When we judge things by their appearances, we often miss something of true value or beauty, something that might have taught us what we needed to know.

Just as we judge others so quickly, we are also afraid of being judged in this way. Yet we need to know that what others think of us is really none of our business. This is so important to understand! You are much larger than people's ideas of who you are, and even your own ideas of who you are. You were sent here by your own Great I AM for a very large purpose. You do not need to save the world or be famous to express this purpose; it could be that your purpose is expressed in being a parent or a good friend or a lover of nature. It has nothing to do with your job, or your worldly status, or your identity.

Who Am I? Why Am I Here?

Your purpose in coming here and having this human experience might be expressed through any number of outer circumstances and experiences. But the purpose is not those outer circumstances and those various coats you wear throughout life: wealthy or poor, married or single or divorced, educated or not educated. You are not any of these things. Discovering your soul's purpose in coming here means first realizing that who you really are is none of these outward things.

So *who are you*? Sometimes it helps to start with understanding what you are not. You are not your job; you are not your status in society; you are not your roles in the family or your accomplishments and failures; you are not your relationship history, your accumulated experiences, your personality, your identity, or your body. You are not what others think of you, good or bad. Keep unpeeling the layers of the onion; peel them back more and more. What are you left with when everything is gone, including your physical body, your name, your face? The intellect can't really do this exercise because you come up against a wall—it must be done in meditation or contemplation. What are you left with when you take away everything you normally think you are? This is the foundation for touching your higher self, your Great I AM—to find that largeness within that is *you* and yet is not limited by any of the things you normally think you are. When you strip away everything inessential, you start to feel your higher self, your Great I AM, your soul.

In a way, it is strange to feel these different centers of gravity, almost like inhabiting two dimensions of reality at once. Yet this shifting into a cosmic or divine perspective is what we humans need to be able to do, at will. We need to become comfortable with shifting dimensions and experiencing the cosmic Light and Love of which we are made and from which we originate.

Seeing with the Eyes of the Universe

I will always remember the first time I really experienced my Great I AM. This moment changed everything for me. I was simply lying down without anything in particular going through my mind, when I was suddenly in a very altered place, a place that had no beginning or end, no light, no sound, no space or time. In this moment, it was if all things made sense, as if all things had a large and profound purpose; all things were exquisitely one unified, cosmic consciousness. There was no weight to my body, as I had no body, no sense of separate self outside the All. It was here in this place I knew that I was not separate from God or Goddess but that I was a part of the very essence that is God and Goddess. I was the Great I AM! In this place, I knew that we all are sparks of this great energy, light, and love that creates all things, time, and events.

In this place of total bliss, I started to recognize, far off in the distance, that I was seeing a planet, a beautiful planet in one of the many spectacular universes. It was so beautiful that I felt a deeper and more profound love than I had ever felt before. I soon recognized this planet as Earth. It was then that my consciousness saw creatures big and small, valleys and mountains, jungles and deserts, and all the life within them. I saw people of all colors, races, and backgrounds from the beginning of time until the present day. It was magnificent and exhilarating. But there was something dreadfully wrong. The human beings were completely unconscious of how beloved they were; they had forgotten that they were indeed creations of Great Spirit themselves. Here before my eyes were such beautiful expressions of Great Spirit, capable of all things, and yet they were blind to their own splendor. Great masses of people were going about their day-to-day lives with no sense of joy, purpose, or meaning.

I saw one man in particular who looked Indian, wearing only a tattered white cloth about his waist as he picked portions of what looked like disregarded mason stones and placed them into a basket, while many others moved about the city on mopeds, bicycles, and on foot. The scene was so sad; everyone had blank expressions on their faces. My consciousness went from city to city, place to place, very quickly, much like flying over the landscape. I also saw myself being born onto this planet to my parents and inhabiting a little, perfect body. I saw glimpses of myself as I grew into an adult and witnessed different aspects of my life that I once saw only as a hindrance. I saw the order of things and how these time periods in my life created great opportunities, lessons, and blessings that shaped me into the woman I am today.

I then witnessed myself in the present moment sitting on the red brick floor of my friend's house in this meditative state. I thought to myself how odd it was to look at myself in real time from another vantage point, not being inside that body on which I was gazing . . . and just like that, the moment my consciousness became self-aware, I was instantly back inside my body. I tried several times to get back to that place, but with no success. I was too much in my mind by then, so I stopped and just reviewed what I had experienced.

The feelings were so intense that I began to tremble and weep for the sheer joy of the experience. I had viewed my life from the time I was born until this present moment and had seen that it was all in divine order. From this experience, I could finally let go of all the judgments

I carried about myself and others, let go of feeling like a victim. I felt a new excitement about life because I was free from the stories of my past. I chose to come to this planet for a reason, not only to experience all this magical beauty around us, to see, hear, touch, and taste life, but also to share and co-create life with other beings. My heart was so full after this experience that I was sure it would burst. I felt utterly changed.

When you experience yourself as the Great I AM, you know that there are no mistakes. Your life is governed by your own higher self, much like a chess piece on a chessboard. My higher self or my Great I AM is the one leading me and guiding me every moment of every day into the situations I encounter to learn lessons and grow as a being. This life is about learning; it's not about earning something or being worthy of God. We are a part of God, not separate!

Spirit has taught me that there is no deity that sent us to this planet, removed our memory of our divine home, and said, "Good luck—I hope you make it back to me, but if you don't, you're going to hell!" We are gods and goddesses who have come here to learn and to grow spiritually. We cannot judge our neighbor for what he or she is going through and what decisions he or she is making, but this is not to say that if we see someone doing something wrong or hurting another, we should turn a blind eye. If we see something wrong, that someone is being hurt, then this becomes part of our experience, and we have a decision to make about how to respond. If you trust your heart and your higher self, you will usually make the right decision—the one that is toward wholeness and integrity.

It is the difficult things in life that teach us and help us grow. Even if you look back on something and say, "I wish I hadn't done that," it was not a mistake; it was a lesson, a learning opportunity, and most likely, you learned something. If we do not learn from the situations our higher selves place before us, then guess what? We'll get to try again! How many times in our lives have we asked ourselves, "Why does this keep happening to me?" Instead of asking why, we might ask, "What is this trying to teach me?"

It is time to remember who you are, to remember that you are greater than you ever thought possible, that it is your higher self governing your life and leading you and guiding you into the situations you experience so that you will learn and grow. It is time to remember why you came here and what gifts you can give to the world at this pivotal time. Every being alive is an expression of the Great I AM, connected to the source of all Love and all Light, the source of Everything. There can be no more reason to think you are small or insignificant—you are more magnificent than you can imagine!

Practice: The Key of Gratitude

One of the most powerful ways to connect with your Great I AM is also one of the most simple. There are feeling states that actually connect us to our hearts and to the entire universe. When you are feeling thankful for all that you have, for the experience of being alive, for the beauty of creation, your entire resonance changes. When you let go of your sense of lacking, your disappointments and unfulfilled desires, you free up a part of your own being that wants to praise existence, to know joy. This is our essential being. You actually come into harmony with the cosmos and unlock the spiritual power of your higher self. Your heart opens and starts to flow correctly. Tears may well up, and you may feel love and tenderness for the little things in your life in ways you haven't for years. Your heart feels light, and you may feel like a child again. Gratitude is that powerful. It is the key that unlocks the door of our own divinity, connecting us through the heart with every-thing else in the universe. We are exalted and purified and feel like the world is new again. It is a powerful antidote to self-pity, depression, and powerlessness. It is very difficult to remember our higher selves when we are mired in feeling like a victim, small and worthless. The feeling of gratitude has the power to raise us up and give us back our intrinsic sense of value and wholeness.

For me, prayer brings me naturally into a state of gratitude. I always start my prayers by thanking Great Spirit and Mother Earth for their blessings, for the blessings of the four directions, for the guidance and nourishment and the gifts I receive every day. It helps me to get very specific about what I am grateful for. Sometimes if we are in our heads, it can take a little while to sink into our feelings again—to feel gratitude. So for me, it can be helpful to name things, to keep speaking of things I am thankful for while my heart attunes and starts to feel itself again. Whether or not you are in the habit of praying in some fashion, you can do this practice of gratitude. Some people are more comfortable with prayer, others with meditation or contemplation. The key is actually to feel gratitude and its related feelings of awe, wonder, tenderness, and joy in your heart.

I have found that focusing on Mother Earth brings people into their hearts (and bodies) very quickly. Because human beings have collectively forgotten about Mother Earth and fallen into a habit of disregard, taking her for granted, I recommend feeling gratitude for Mother Earth every day as an antidote to this collective wound. To feel gratitude for Mother Earth, for plants, animals, and insects, for the waters and winds and the sunshine and the soil, is to feel gratitude for our human bodies, which are also Earth. For too long, we have disregarded what a sacred gift it is to be here, alive, on Mother Earth, to have these precious human bodies. Somehow, cultivating an attitude of gratitude to Mother Earth helps connect us to the root of ourselves. It is healing for her and healing for us.

But rather than focusing on something general or abstract, such as "Mother Earth," you may need to focus on something concrete to bring forth your feelings of gratitude. I like to start with a particular thing. Whatever you feel most grateful for in your life, you can start with that. It could be your child's face in the morning, it could be your pet, it could be a particularly beautiful sunrise you once witnessed that made you remember the beauty of this world, it could be a small flower—whatever arouses your feelings of love and thankfulness, focus on that. At first, it is often necessary to focus on things seemingly outside yourself, but the task is to gradually expand your focus to include more and more of the world—other human beings and yourself.

Ultimately, when you can feel gratitude and love for other specific human beings and for yourself—for everything that you are and aren't—you are on your way to unlocking the secret of the cosmos. When you can feel gratitude for all of existence, even the painful and confusing aspects of it, and for those parts of yourself and others with which you may struggle, then you are stepping into cosmic reality: all is Love. Every human being on planet Earth today is being asked to realize this. Gratitude is one of the most potent keys to opening the doors of the heart and the Great I AM. If you are ever faced with chaos and uncertainty around you, try to remain grateful for something. This will open your connection to your higher self and help you navigate the choppy waters more effectively and in harmony with your soul's purpose.

Letting Go of Expectations

We humans are a funny species. We are always emotionally and mentally stuck on what we are lacking or on what is wrong in the moment: our love lives or our jobs are not fulfilling, or our relationships are not meeting our expectations. The problem is that we have expectations, and therefore we set ourselves up for failure and disappointment. I have struggled with expectations in my life, and now that I work publicly and have taken on more responsibility, I am always having to learn further lessons about expectations, mostly about how not to have them and how not to worry about fulfilling them.

I was taught something important about expectations by a great man named Lhaka Lama when I was in Sweden in 2010. He had arranged to come to visit me before my talk, having heard that I was visiting Sweden, where he lives. Knowing he was a Tibetan lama, I was nervous and self-conscious meeting him, and my expectations put me in an anxious state of mind before he even arrived. To my relief, he came to the door dressed in normal street clothes. He introduced himself casually, with no ego or pretense, and simply sat down on the couch and called me to sit beside him. I offered him some chocolates, and he ate them in his calm, quiet, and joyful manner. He was totally relaxed in himself.

I learned a great deal just from being in his presence. He told me that I should give no energy to expectation—that my job in this world is to live simply in Love in the best way I can and to allow others to live in their own way. I was getting ready to address several hundred people during one of my presentations, and I was nervous. He knew this, and with a little pat on my chest, he told me to relax my heart. He told me that it was not my job to convince people to believe me or the message I shared but simply to share the message. Then he told me something I will never forget: "Your job is to cast the stone into the water. You're not in charge of how many ripples form, or how big the ripples in the water are after casting the stone." He spoke of how expectations are what lead us into despair as well as into feelings of doubt, failure, and judgment of others.

His words have stayed with me ever since. When I feel the all-encompassing pressure of trying to fulfill others' or my own expectations, or of getting caught up in how others think of me, I am reminded of his analogy of tossing the stone and not having expectations. This is so important to remember so that we do not judge others or ourselves. We cannot control how what we say or do will be received or what will come afterward. We can only speak and act from our soul's deepest urgings, toward the highest good. Whether we are loved or hated, whether our efforts come to success or failure, we can do our best to free ourselves from attachment and expectation. This is an important step in transforming those limiting thought patterns that would prevent us from fulfilling our soul's purpose here. Every day I try to release the fear of what could happen in the future and simply stay grounded in my deepest knowing about what I am here to do and share. Every day, I try to not have expectations and to do what my heart wants most, even though it is sometimes difficult.

When you free yourself of expectations, of how things are supposed to be and how they are meant to turn out, you free yourself to be fully alive in each moment, following the callings of your spirit.

Changing the Channel

With so many catastrophic events happening in the world today and so much uncertainty about the future, it is crucial to be aware of the negativity that we allow ourselves to take in. This can profoundly affect our ability to stay connected to our hearts at those times when we most need to stay connected. We unconsciously feed on images of fear and destruction, and it ends up making us more passive, more powerless, more disconnected from Spirit and our higher selves. The media, in particular, uses images of destruction and chaos to keep people glued to their TVs and computers—they like to create a web of fear because fear keeps people tuned in. Although it is hard to see death and destruction and not give in to fear and despair, that is exactly what we need to be able to do now. We need to be able to recognize those moments when we are giving our energy away to negativity and *change the channel*.

It's easy to get drawn into fear and pessimism about the future. The gulf oil spill and the Fukushima nuclear disaster in Japan are two recent horrific events that sent the whole world into a state of fear. I don't think there was anyone who saw these things happening who did not feel sorrowful, scared, and worried. This is natural; it is human to feel grief and compassion in response to suffering. But there is a way to feel compassion and emotion and still not give your energy away to negativity, which affects your energy field. You can make a choice about how you inwardly respond when faced with outer adversity or chaos. You can choose to stay tuned to the higher vibrations of the heart and, in this way, change your reality. Do you wish to live in heaven or in hell? Both are available to us in each moment, regardless of what our outer reality looks like. We can always choose what inner state to be in, regardless of what we see outside of us. If we can do this, we can change not only what we experience individually—we can actually change the world.

When I have spoken to people around the world about "changing the channel," I have often been asked whether I am saying that we should not pay attention to the news or what is going on in the world. This is definitely not what I mean. We need to be aware of what is happening in the world, to be actively engaged in working for change as our hearts dictate—but we do not need to accept and absorb the negativity that is constantly being fed to us from so many directions. To *change the channel* means that you do not seek out things or attach to things that make you feel bad, low, anxious, fearful, confused, or small. You can focus on something beautiful, positive, inspiring, or hopeful instead, and thus protect your energy from being lowered. Otherwise, you actually create more negativity just by focusing on it and giving it so much of your attention and emotion. You cannot help solve a problem or crisis by becoming depressed and fearful or by replaying in your mind just how bad it is. To create something better, you need to be in your highest energy as a divine co-creator, to be connected to your higher self, your heart.

Television and the Internet are two of the most powerful forces in our lives wherein we passively absorb a great deal of garbage without being aware of it. The cumulative effect of this is that our feelings about ourselves and the world are actually affected. Absorbing so much mental information of a low vibration does exactly the opposite of what time spent with nature does: it depletes your energy field. You get stuck in your head, and your attention is drawn in a million directions, all unimportant and shallow. More and more of us have grown to depend on computers and high-tech gadgets, and I'm no exception, but the more we can limit our passive exposure to such meaningless chatter, the better. If you hear something negative on the news, realize that you can change the channel. The key here is not to check out and be unaware of things but to recognize that you need not live in fear or accept someone else's version of reality and of what is possible (or impossible). You do not have to give your energy to negativity, regardless of what is occurring around you or across the world. You have an obligation to protect your most powerful creative resource: your own consciousness. You can choose to focus on that which is life giving, hopeful, nourishing, inspiring, and toward healing and wholeness.

This is true in more everyday situations, as well. If someone with you is speaking harshly of someone else, or spewing a lot of cynicism and negativity, don't be afraid to ask the person to change the channel, or simply refuse to participate in that kind of negative conversation. You can stop listening or attempt to steer the conversation to something more positive. Likewise, when we get pulled into mindless consumerism, we are also consuming much negativity. We are usually being unconsciously manipulated to think that we need things that we don't actually need. Instead of using our creative powers to create happiness and beauty for ourselves and others, we are told that we can buy these things and that without them, we will be lost. We give away our power this way.

If you catch yourself sinking into this mind space and notice that your feelings are being channeled toward buying this, that, or the other thing, you can decide to change the channel. Instead of buying that fancy new gadget, you can build something, paint, write a poem, play with a child, or take a hike in the mountains. You can do something that actually gives you more life energy and not just take the quick-fix high that buying stuff gives. Giving our energy away to consumerism and things that drain us causes us to forget how spiritually powerful and free we really are—that what we might have and create is far beyond the momentary happiness that such distractions give to our lives. None of these things are bad, but when we get caught up in them, we become lessened—and unknowingly give away our power and life energy.

Every morning and each night, look into the sky and truly feel and affirm: "Everything is good and beautiful. I am a creator; I am God and Goddess. I can change my world." Doing so will raise your energy vibration sky high. When you read something in the newspaper and get wrapped up in fearful negativity, your energy plummets. It's the difference between being in charge of your state of being, your consciousness, and being a slave to whatever is outside of you. You always have a choice.

This past year, I had great opportunity to practice changing the channel in my own life. Becoming well known does have its disadvantages. I have been blessed that my online videos have reached millions of people, and the overwhelming majority of these people are extremely loving and supportive. But with a lot of light and goodness always comes some darkness, too. I found to my dismay that when I had reached a certain level of recognition, some individuals began attacking me and spreading blatantly false, even ridiculous, statements about me online. At first, I tried to engage these people in the spirit of good will and truth, but I soon realized that some people will ridicule you no matter what you say or do. It is an unfortunate reality that for every person who tries to speak or act in the world, who steps into visibility, there will be a person who wants to throw stones and criticize. At first, this kept me up at night. Then I realized that I was giving away a great deal of my energy and power. The only way to conquer such negativity is by holding a vibration of love and compassion, regardless of what comes. If you meet it with defensiveness or anger, it only gives the negative more power. Though it has not always been easy, I have had to become adept at changing the channel to be able to go on and continue my work for the sake of Mother Earth and not be intimidated or swayed from my path. I had to commit to the truth of my being and to stand firm in what I know to be my soul's purpose. I had to stop focusing on the negative and hold on to the positive—in other words, I had to change my channel.

As human beings, we sometimes think that if we are good and loving, and do everything right, we will not face criticism or hostility from others. But this is not always the case. We live in the dimension of duality, where darkness and light coexist. We are sometimes met with negativity for no apparent reason. We do not have to accept the negativity others direct at us. Sometimes even the people closest to us may try to undermine or belittle us to feel better about themselves. This is mostly unconscious behavior and always has to do with that person doing the judging, not the person who is being judged. We can change the channel and not allow the negative projections and judgments of others to make us smaller.

We can remember that we are a spark of divine Love, and that we are perfect as we are. No one has the right or the power to make us small, to take our energy—only we can give our energy away. It is so much better to give our energy to that which inspires our hearts and enlarges our sense of who we are and our capabilities. It may not always be easy, but it is one of the tools that will help us awaken as human beings, especially when we are faced with destruction and fear. Instead of taking it in, we can turn inward and choose to stay connected to Love.

Your Speech Has Power

Human beings were given a powerful gift that no other creature on Earth has been given: the power of language. Animals are communicating all the time, with each other and with us, but communicating with words is the sole province of human beings. With our words, we are able to create in a very special way. The Bible says, "In the beginning was the Word . . . and the Word was God." It was understood that the Word could create. In fact, it is our ability to give voice to our thoughts and feelings that gives birth to the entire human experience. Yet most of us take this gift for granted and do not understand the power our words have to create or destroy.

We are at a time on planet Earth when we are being increasingly faced with chaos, change, and destruction. Unfortunately, we have become addicted to what the media tells us is real and passively absorb the cynicism and fear that are being fed to us through language to keep us in a state of dependency. Although it is easy to buy in to this and to continue to parrot cynicism, negativity, and fear in how we speak, we must become actively aware of the power of our speech again. We must refuse to speak about, even think about, our world in the way we have been taught. We can allow for a new vision to emerge and let our speech call that new vision into being. We can see destruction happening and respond to it from our hearts, yet insist on seeing not only destruction but potential creation. This is the trick—this is what I have been shown is so important for human beings to do now. Do not focus on the eye of the storm but see beyond it, to the rainbow on the horizon that can only come by letting the old things die away. Whatever we are faced with, we can see an opportunity and a hope, or we can see destruction, chaos, and meaninglessness. This determines the reality in which we will live.

Our voices are our vibrations, and so we must be aware of whether the energy behind our words is destructive or constructive. Whatever words you speak, you give your energy to them. If you speak of death, destruction, fear, chaos, or scarcity, you are also thinking and imagining those things, probably in great detail. On some level, we have a choice. We can become conscious of what we are imagining and of that to which we are giving our energy, even before we speak. You actually can stop a train of thought in process and refuse to go there. You can change the channel and look at reality differently. This is the key to imagining and bringing about a new future for humanity. When faced with one apparent reality, we need to be able to envision something different, to make it so by our commitment, by our words and speech, and by our spiritual intentions.

This is true on a personal level, as well. The words we use create positive and negative outcomes in our individual lives. To gossip is not only a waste of vital energy, which makes us smaller, but the negativity we generate attaches to us as well as to the people of whom we are speaking. Because energy always flows both ways, what we put out in the world will be reflected back to us—we can be sure that if we are critical and ungenerous with others, we will feel that way ourselves, or already do. Lack of generosity to others usually masks a lack of generosity toward oneself. If someone is gossiping to a group of friends, the energy of each person in the group plummets. It lowers everyone's vibration. Yet if we are in this situation, we can choose to actively change it. We can change the channel, change the energy, by using the power of our words. We can say something positive about the person being attacked, even something small. This requires actually digging deeper and finding your own generosity of heart, to see the person differently, not just making something up to be nice. Simply by saying something positive and truly feeling it, you stop the negative spiral by bringing a generous and compassionate spirit into the room.

Though we cannot control what others say around us, or to us, we can change the effect that others' words have on us. This is important because what others say to us or about us can change how we feel about ourselves and can disempower us, if we let it. Let's say you are walking down the road, and someone who is very agitated and angry flips you off and yells, "Watch out, you fat cow!" Do you allow these words to enter you? Do you accept them as truth? Too often, we let the words of others haunt us and become true for us; we carry them around in our heads all our lives, even if they are shouted in anger and come from a stranger.

We need to understand that we have the power either to accept or not accept those words others use about us. You have a choice in how to react to verbal negativity. Ninety-nine percent of the time, human beings react in kind to the energy that comes at them. If someone pays you a compliment and uses kindness and love in his or her words, most likely, you will say something very kind back. Yet if someone shouts something negative at you, 99 percent of the time, you will react in anger or defensiveness, and the negative energy just grows and grows. We have all seen how this can spiral out of control. Yet as conscious beings who understand the power of our words and speech, we can do our best to alter the situation, to refuse to use our words for destruction and get drawn into a negative reaction.

Because love is the strongest energy, it will always win in the end. If someone is yelling at you or putting you down, if you choose not to accept their words and say something kind in return, you will change the energy from negative to positive. Even if, in that moment, the person who initially shouted in anger doesn't know how to react to your kindness and again says something rude, the person will walk away with your words in his or her mind, and they will have an effect!

The words we use are especially powerful with our children. How often do we parents become angry or just plain exhausted and shout at our kids to be quiet. Or we say, "Stop that dancing around, you're making me nuts!" The child may have been attempting to express herself, and what she hears from the parent is a powerful prohibition that could prevent her from expressing herself freely in the future. This was certainly not what was intended!

When we speak negatively, we are literally impressing on reality an image; if our words are repeated often enough, even inwardly, reality will begin to conform to our words. If I mention to a friend, "Things never work out well for me," I am basically instructing reality how to respond to my efforts, especially if they are backed by emotions that have become habitual and unconscious. I am damning my efforts to failure. Likewise, if I speak to my friend and say, "I just know this will work out perfectly," I am allowing for this to happen and paving the way toward success. In this sense, our words have an almost magical power to construct our reality.

When you speak with positivity, sincerity, generosity, and beauty, and you honor your word with commitment, others will respond to you with trust, openness, and respect. You clear a path for beautiful and positive things to come to you because you are actively attracting them with your every word. What you put out will come back to you energetically. Knowing that what you say and in what manner you say it to others will be reflected back at you, you can start to create the world of kindness and love you want around you by speaking, as much as possible, with love and kindness.

When I go places to speak, many people are obviously concerned about what will happen in 2012. They are rightfully concerned about whether the magnetic poles of the Earth will shift and what that might mean for their families, communities, and everyday lives. When answering such questions, I am very aware that I must choose my words carefully. Though I may have been shown certain images and Earth changes that will happen, I am careful not to present these to others as real (they may be my reality, but each person must decide what is real for him or her) or to speak of things in a way that would create fear. This is crucial, because how we use our consciousness right now is of the utmost importance. We can affect the future by our mass human consciousness right now, and fear only helps to create fearful situations. We may not change, ultimately, what is meant to happen on planet Earth, but *how* it happens is being created day by day, moment by moment. This is why no one can foresee exactly what will happen on Earth, and when. In some ways, the future exists already, and in some ways, it doesn't. We are creating it right now! Therefore we should all actively envision and speak of the highest good, of the highest beauty, and above all, of what we wish to create.

If we all do this—envision a new Earth based on Love as the highest principle governing human beings—we will help the cosmos in creating it. If we speak only Love and of a high vibration, we will create that higher vibration on Earth. We will build up our collective spiritual power and summon it for the purpose of creation, reclaiming our divine gifts as human beings.

The Awakening of the Sacred Feminine

For a very long time now, there has been an unmistakable imbalance on Earth in the way human societies work and in the way we relate to each other. Human society has been driven by power, mind, and force for millennia, and for much of human history, women have been treated no better than chattel, as property to be owned, coveted, controlled, and dominated. So-called feminine qualities, such as tenderness, compassion, receptivity, cooperation, and humility, have been viewed as weak and as inferior to so-called masculine qualities such as competitiveness, aggression, dominance, individualism, and self-sufficiency. Men, and masculine qualities, have controlled the values and the organization of human society for so long that it seems like the natural order of things; we cannot remember a time when it was different. Yet the problem is not the masculine qualities but the imbalance between the masculine and feminine. It is time for a major change.

The problem is the imbalanced masculine, not masculinity itself. This is where mind, ego, and power rule over the heart and feeling—where the body is not valued and cherished, and living things are seen as separate from spirit, the divine, the sacred. Softness, gentleness, receptivity, love, humility, and compassion are not valued, while competitiveness, force, individuality, greed, and ego are valued and rewarded. If you look around, you'll see that the treatment of women and the treatment of Mother Earth have gone hand in hand. Both have been disrespected and abused, and their true gifts, power, and beauty have been suppressed and controlled. We are in a state of imbalance that is killing Mother Earth and making humanity sick. The feminine wisdom and power, which in many ways is the power of unconditional *love,* long kept down and dormant, must rise again to lead us back into balance.

The Role of Men and the Masculine

The feminine does not mean only women; it lives in men, as well, and men have a special role to play. The sacred feminine qualities will blossom in men's hearts just as much as in women's, and many men already embody the feminine qualities in balance with masculine qualities. The role of the masculine in relation to the sacred feminine is very important. For many men, it will mean becoming protectors and tender stewards of the feminine—of the Earth, of women, of children, of that which is soft and innocent and vulnerable. Men will use their strength, their will, and their minds to serve the sacred balance of life, to serve Love, to act from their hearts, knowing the great beauty they are helping to protect, restore, and care for.

The masculine will be restored to its sacred and essential place when it is reconnected to the heart and recognizes its ancient longing to serve and protect the sacred feminine. These men will be fully connected to their emotions and will be warriors of Love, strong and capable and courageous. They will not need to dominate or be driven by ego and control. They will gladly work in the background and allow the feminine to regain her voice and share her wisdom. They will be open to receiving and listening, not just to speaking and actively doing. This is not just a fantasy, this is what will happen and must happen on planet Earth for there to be balance and harmony.

In truth, both the masculine and the feminine are in need of deep healing if we are to come to balance on planet Earth. In 2009, during the Return of the Ancestors ceremony we did in Santa Fe, the entire second day was devoted to healing the wounds of the masculine and feminine. I was terrified beforehand about having to lead this part of the ceremony because I myself had much healing to do in these areas. What transpired showed me just how deep these sexual and gender wounds go, in men and in women, and how this may be the most important aspect of healing that any of us have to do. What the experience of this ceremony also showed me is that we cannot speak about healing the feminine, and the rise of the sacred feminine in the world, without speaking about Mother Earth.

Mother Earth as the Divine Feminine

If we want to awaken and heal the feminine, we first need to have a relationship with Mother Earth. The Earth truly is our mother. When most people think of "mother," they think of being taken care, of tenderness. There is nothing a good mother wouldn't give her children. She will give food before she takes food; she will run into a burning building to save her children. She will do everything for her child. She is the epitome of tenderness and love. She gives life and nurtures life, even with no thanks and no reward for doing so. This is exactly how Mother Earth is for us human beings. Every breath we take is from her; every meal we eat is given from her; this flesh, these miraculous bodies in which we exist, are a gift from her. Yet how often do we thank her or acknowledge the gift of this life? Most people in the Western world are taught to pray to the Father—and many religions teach this. But how many people are taught to pray to Mother Earth, to thank her and love her like one's own mother, to go to her for help? In the religion in which I was raised, Mother is never mentioned. The feminine was erased from the religion entirely. This neglect has been a huge loss and a vast mistake for human beings, cleaved as we are to our Mother every moment our lives in the most basic way.

I do not mean to imply that Mother Earth (or the feminine, for that matter) is always sweet and gentle in some sentimental, idealized way. Mother Earth can be destructive and angry. She can be impartial. Death is part of her reality, and pain and suffering are, as well. Yet she is the Everything in which we have our lives and our breath. Just as we could not be here on planet Earth if a woman did not bear us, we could not be alive for one second if Mother Earth did not provide for us—earth, air, fire, water—and hold us in life with her breath. If Mother Earth grows ill, we grow ill. If any one part of her dies or sickens, we will grow sick and die. That is the reality of our plight here on Earth—yet astoundingly, we proceed as if this were not the case!

Loving Mother Earth goes hand in hand with bringing the feminine and masculine back into balance, with loving and valuing the feminine qualities in men and women. The two are not separate. Yet I feel that we do best to start by loving and connecting to Mother Earth, who to me is the Divine Feminine, a goddess worthy of our love and tenderness and respect. I think it is easier this way—to start by connecting in love to Mother Earth—because this softens our hearts naturally and helps our energy flow in healthful ways. The more balanced we each become, the easier it is to open our hearts and work on our deep wounds of sex and gender. Mother Earth to me *is* the sacred feminine—and without the sacred feminine being seated on her throne again, being awakened and restored in the world, we will not continue as a species. I have been told that Mother Earth is sacred to all beings in the Universe—she is a paradise unparalleled, a being of enthralling beauty. The Universe will not allow human beings to destroy her. Yet we still are harming and raping her—and unless we shift the human consciousness dramatically, we will continue on this path to our own destruction.

Honoring Love, Beauty, and the Feminine Qualities of Soul

Many of us are waking up to the fact that what is most tender, beautiful, loving, and humble must be respected and honored again in our world. The quality of Love must become the ruling quality, that for which we strive and measure things by. We must weep for all we have done to our mother and pray to her with our most sincere hearts, sending her our love and gratitude for the gift of our lives. It is important to feel this love sincerely and connect with her energetically each day. She has saved my life in the past and can save yours, too, when you are suffering or in need. She is the essence of compassion and love. The wisdom of the feminine will rise again in the world—and with it, women will take positions of leadership in guiding us back to balance, not simply replacing men with women but replacing a style of leadership based on separateness, individualism, greed, control, and ego with one that is based on cooperation, harmony, compassion, caring, and generosity.

The sacred feminine also includes the quality of beauty. You cannot appreciate the feminine without appreciating the quality of beauty. I do not mean what is judged beautiful to the eye but to realize the deeper beauty in things, that which delights the heart and gives life meaning. If we were really to see and appreciate the beauty of our Mother Earth, we would be full of praise and weep with gratitude. We would be filled with ecstasy just to be alive. This is the state in which we need to live: filled with gratitude, wonder, and awe and willing to do anything to save her, to see her restored to her throne. When the sacred feminine ascends her throne, this Earth will become a paradise again. I intend for us all to see that day.

Mother is the most profound word you can say. The words *love* and *mother* are the highest vibrating words in existence. When the word *mother* has been spoken, I have seen how the energy skyrockets. This is because for most of us, the word *love* and the word *mother* contain the same frequency of energy, regardless of what kind of mother we have had. You might even say that these are the words that are closest to our hearts from our first to our last breath.

Without Mother, nothing would exist. It is always said that behind every great man, there is a woman. But behind every great woman, there is also a woman. We are all born of a woman, a mother. Mother is everything. Every breath you take, every ounce of water you drink, every meal you have ever eaten, every beautiful thing you have seen, every friend and loved one you have ever had has been given to you by Mother. For too long, we have thrown away the feminine, the Mother. Mother Earth cannot become her heavenly, high self until her own children recognize her as the Divine Feminine itself, a being of great tenderness, wisdom, and boundless Love.

The feminine is where we learn the qualities of tenderness, compassion, beauty, and love. Without the return of the feminine, we will continue to go to war and kill each other, to deny the needs of others and the realities of others' suffering, and focus on protecting only ourselves and our own needs. The feminine is the one thing that can save us because it reflects a changing of the heart. In the future, instead of saying, "I'll get mine, you go get yours," we will say, "Let's take care of each other and help each other." Let's not kill each other because we believe differently; let's sit down and talk. If the waters are dirty, what can we do together to clean them? How can we feed everyone? The Mother says, let's feed everyone so no one is left out, no child is hungry. The feminine will take care of the elderly, the children, the animals, to restore balance to the sacred circle of life.

We have two parents: Great Spirit and Mother Earth, sacred Mother and sacred Father. Sacred Father gives us our spirit, and Sacred Mother gives us our bodies. If we were just spirits, we would not be here; we couldn't interact with each other and have this blessed experience of existence on Earth. We must thank Mother for letting us have our precious human bodies so that we may experience this great mystery of human life, every emotion we've ever felt, every beauty we've ever glimpsed, every beloved we've ever held to us, in bliss. Without Mother, nothing exists. Even Great Spirit was born of Mother—she gives birth to everything!

A Special Ceremony for the Sacred Feminine

In October 2010, I traveled to Eureka Springs, Arkansas, to speak. Although I didn't know it until the last minute, I was actually being sent there to conduct what would be a very special ceremony for the awakening of the sacred feminine and the healing of the sacred waters. Jennifer, who usually assisted me on my travels, was coming, but I was told by Spirit that, this time, she was to help me conduct the ceremony, representing and summoning the sacred feminine in a special way. I asked her to chronicle the events leading up to the trip as well as the ceremony itself. It turned out to be quite beautiful, and I have asked her to share her notes about the experience to give you a sense of the actual flow and energy of this powerful ceremony—and how Spirit communicates to me about what needs to happen, how, and when.

Jennifer's Notes: The 10/10/10 in Eureka Springs, Arkansas

One of the first invitations Kiesha received in her first year as shaman was from Marie, a woman in Arkansas who was putting together a Healing Path Expo the weekend of October 10, 2010, in Eureka Springs, Arkansas. Whenever Kiesha would receive such invitations, especially in the beginning, she would feel things out, meditate, and see how easily things came together. Everything around the Healing Expo flowed positively, and logistics came smoothly and easily. Kiesha accepted the invitation. I knew 10/10/10 was an important date, and I wondered why she was being sent to Arkansas of all places. Neither of us had been to Arkansas, but we knew it would be an adventure.

The weekend before, Kiesha had a two-day workshop in Santa Fe with sixty people. In the morning of the second day of the workshop, she woke up feeling strange—"between the worlds," as she put it. Then, on our way to the workshop, she got a nosebleed. This often happened before she was about to receive information or a message from Spirit. We were in the parking lot sitting in the car when she started to get a message. Though I could not hear the voice, Kiesha was clearly being asked questions and would answer yes or no or would ask for clarification. I grabbed a piece of paper and a pen and got ready to transcribe whatever was coming through.

When the communication ended, Kiesha told me that it had been a male voice speaking to her. He asked her if she understood the significance of "10/10/10." She answered yes somewhat uncertainly and was told that she should learn more about it because it was very important. He told Kiesha that we were to bring a specific quartz crystal to Arkansas. He described in detail Kiesha's stone, which had a horizontal cut in its center. He also said to bring a small, pink quartz crystal in my care that represented the sacred feminine. And we were to bring yet another crystal, the one "in its tapestry," which was also in my care. The first two would be placed in the Earth and left in Arkansas, and the third, the one "in its tapestry," would return home with me.

After some puzzling, we figured out that this last crystal he mentioned was a very special crystal, given to me several years ago by Kiesha that I always kept on my altar in its embroidered case. It was a double-sided, wine-colored Tibetan quartz wrapped in copper wire, a powerful conductor crystal. This crystal would absorb the energies of what we were to do there and return home with us. That evening after the workshop, we were able to locate the exact crystals that Spirit described in detail from among our crystals—these small crystals would play a significant role in what Spirit knew would happen in Arkansas.

In the next week, Kiesha received additional information about what she was to do in Arkansas. I was to play an active role in the ceremony and be responsible for placing the small rose quartz crystal in the ground. This would represent the sacred feminine. The two crystals we would place in the Earth were to be touching each other. They would connect with the other crystals around the world that would be awakening on 10/10/10. We learned that a powerful activation of Atlantean crystals would be happening on Mount Magazine in Arkansas.

Northwest central Arkansas, where we would be, holds one of the highest crystal concentrations in the world. Some of the most powerful Atlantean master crystals were buried under Mount Magazine and were about to be awakened on this triple portal date of 10/10/10. Powerful energies would activate from deep within the Earth at that time, bringing humanity collectively closer to spiritual ascension. Now I knew why we were heading to Arkansas.

Kiesha was to lead the ceremony at 10:10 A.M. on 10/10/10 in Eureka Springs, where sacred healing waters had always flowed. The placing of the crystals would not only help activate the return of the sacred feminine to the planet but would help in healing the waters of the region. In a vision, Kiesha saw us leading everyone in the circle in toning, sending our souls' tones into the crystals.

When we arrived at the camp where the expo was being held, in the beautiful Ozarks, we noticed the gentle, soft, life-abundant energy of the place. Animals were everywhere. Bees, locusts, and butterflies buzzed all around the little cabin where we were staying. The trees and plants seemed to envelope us in lush beauty. Each night, we laid out our crystals on the Earth under the starry sky and moonlight and said prayers over them, thanking Great Spirit and Mother Earth and asking Mother to bless the crystals for the healing and awakening of the planet. There was a feeling of peace and blessing all weekend. The anticipation for Sunday was gathering in everyone. People had been instructed to bring their crystals with them to the ceremony, and there was a palpable excitement about what would happen on this most powerful spiritual date.

The day before the ceremony, Kiesha had walked the land, barefooted, to try to locate the place where the ceremony should be. She had finally found the place, where two ley lines intersected. She could feel the Earth energy emanating up through her feet and was able to find the large, energetic bands that ran north–south and east–west. We marked off the perimeter of the circle and the center of the circle where the two ley lines intersected. This was where the crystals would be placed in the Earth.

On Sunday morning, about a hundred people gathered in the large circle we had marked out and then became quiet and reverent, creating a focused environment for the sacred to be summoned. Kiesha fully entered her role as shaman, Little Grandmother, and began preparing the sacred ground of the circle. Starting at the north point of the circle, she moved around the circle, smudging each person and any crystal he or she was holding with burning sage. After this, from the center of the circle, she offered prayers to the Four Directions, to Great Spirit, and to Mother Earth. As she knelt and prayed to Mother Earth, we could feel everyone's heart opening as people touched and knelt on the Earth for this special, tender prayer. Many were moved to tears.

Then Little Grandmother placed a symbolic person in each direction point to anchor the energy: a woman, born in Arkansas, in the north; a man, also born in Arkansas, in the south; a grandmother in the west; and a grandfather in the east. She then poured some water from a nearby sacred spring into the Earth to mark the place where the crystals would be placed. It was then that she received guidance from Spirit to blow tobacco smoke into each person's third eye, a place of connection to Great Spirit, and navel, the place of connection to Mother Earth.

So under a blazing sun, she started at the north and worked her way around the circle, blowing smoke into each person's forehead and belly, while everyone held a crystal in his or her right hand. Left hands were to be placed over bellies. By the time Little Grandmother had completed one-quarter of the large circle, she was starting feeling altered. She needed to be somewhat between the worlds to listen to guidance from Spirit, yet she also needed to stay present and grounded to conduct ceremony, while leaving nothing out.

Standing in the center of the circle, she explained the significance of the ceremony—how the crystals would help activate and awaken the sacred feminine and heal the sacred waters here. She said we were given the task of moving from the mind and ego back into the heart and that we needed to remember and love Mother Earth and the Divine Feminine. She spoke of how even "Great Spirit could not be born without the feminine," how important it was for the feminine to be seated on her throne and assume her rightful place in the world again. At several points, people called out with emotion—affirming the truth of her statements. You could feel the emotion building, and people were passionately moved by this vision of the return of the sacred feminine. Little Grandmother spoke poignantly of how it was not some big, flashy crystal that was chosen to represent the sacred feminine but a small, unobtrusive pink crystal.

While she spoke, I held the small, curved rose quartz crystal in my hand. Little Grandmother ended with the words "and now we will honor Her" and sat down inside the circle. I knew it was time for me to speak. I stood and held up my small crystal. My emotion broke through as I spoke with my eyes closed, praying that all beings might know that they are beloved, that they are Love, that what has been excluded and forgotten might be remembered and brought back into wholeness—that Earth might become a paradise again, and that beauty be awakened in all hearts.

Then, as Little Grandmother had foreseen, we asked everyone to imagine the vibration of heart-melting, unconditional love and to bring forth the tone that for each person vibrated this love. We asked them to direct their unique soul sounds into the crystal. Slowly, the tones began to rise as a harmony of voices emerged. Some of the women's voices seemed to drift upward into angelic tones. For fifteen minutes or so, we toned into the crystals. Finally, Little Grandmother began praying again and asked me to place my curved crystal so that it fit into the notch of her larger crystal. We fastened them together with red strips of fabric. She then poured the remaining sacred spring water over them and smudged them. Then Little Grandmother offered a blessing of the four elements of earth, air, fire, and water, which she had been guided to use by Spirit.

Little Grandmother took a shovel and made the first dent where the hole would be dug. After saying a few prayers quietly together, I placed the crystal bundle into the hole. Little Grandmother placed a handful of Earth over it while saying prayers, after which everyone from the circle was invited to come forward and finish covering the crystals with Earth.

She asked everyone present to give their crystals, which now contained the prayers and vibrations of the ceremony, back to Mother Earth by placing them in wild water. This would help conduct the vibration of love we had toned into the crystals far and wide because water is the fastest conductor of energy. These crystals would not only help heal the waters but as the water evaporated, the prayers and vibrations we had invested in them would be carried into the air, then rain down on everything, blessing Mother Earth and connecting potently with the other crystals in the area that were awakening.

As we all slowly left the circle, we felt that something truly cosmic in significance had taken place. Our hearts overflowed with gratitude and joy to have taken part in this momentous ceremony together. As we slowly broke from the circle, many people knelt one by one on the Earth and said prayers over the crystals, touching the Earth with deep reverence. It was a beautiful scene—one I will never forget. I think everyone present truly felt connected as one heart, one family. I know that every face that afternoon was radiating a beautiful light!

The Importance of Crystals

Crystals are truly amazing gifts from Mother Earth. They hold more power than we can possibly realize. In the distant past, human beings understood the true power and uses of crystals. I have been shown that in the time of Atlantis, between 40,000 and 10,000 B.C., human beings used crystals for energy to power their cities and their homes, to heal diseases and psychological imbalances, for communication, and for spiritual advancement and creation. The smallest quartz crystal can store and conduct a vast amount of knowledge and energy. This is because crystals are actually living beings and have a consciousness. Today we are just beginning to tap into the potentials of crystals in our technologies, especially in computers. We know that quartz crystal holds memory. It can be programmed to hold a particular frequency and conduct spiritual energy and intentions. It can amplify and store spiritual knowledge and teachings. If humanity knew the full potential of crystals, we would be astounded. They play a huge role in our advancement as a species and in the future of our Earth right now. For the past few years, powerful crystals that were used and programmed at the time of Atlantis are again awakening to help Mother Earth and humanity move into a higher dimension.

After I became Little Grandmother, I was entrusted with seven very special crystals. These crystals, I was told, were used in the time of Atlantis. Now they were being given to different wisdom keepers on the planet so that they could be reopened and placed back within Mother Earth. They would need to be placed in particular locations on the planet where powerful ley lines crossed to strengthen the energy grid on Mother Earth before her Great Shift. I was told that these crystals had been given to the Atlantean priests by star beings, with instructions on how to use them. Each one holds a different cosmic energy and purpose. At the time of the fall of Atlantis, they were shut down so that they would not be misused. They were kept safe by the pure-hearted priests who left Atlantis before it sank. The crystals were saved for this time, when Mother Earth would shift into a higher dimension and human beings would have the opportunity to shift with her.

These crystals carry not only Mother Earth energy but also cosmic energy of a higher frequency. When these crystals are opened and placed in one of Mother Earth's arteries, this higher frequency spreads throughout the Earth, connecting the sacred power places of the Earth. There are higher-dimensional energies pouring down to Earth now from the heavens, and these energies become activated within the crystals, supercharging Mother Earth's energy grid. Wisdom keepers have been placing these special crystals in specific places around the Earth over the last three years. Interestingly, scientists have reported that within the last three years, the human body's energy field as well as that of the Earth is now vibrating faster than it ever has before.

When these crystals came into my possession, I was told that further instruction would come through Mother Spirit, my primary guide, on where each would need to be placed. I had to make an oath that I would never choose where they would go but that I would wait for specific instructions. As of today, I have placed four of these crystals back into Mother Earth, in northern New Mexico, among the redwoods of California, in Maui, and in Sweden. Some of these crystal ceremonies have been public, and some have been private, depending on the circumstances surrounding my visit to each of these places. The returning of these crystals to Mother Earth has been one of my most sacred tasks since I became Little Grandmother. I am still awaiting instructions for the last three crystals as of this writing.

The Crystal Ceremonies for Mother Earth

In Santa Fe, the Opening of Ancient Anasazi Lands

The first crystal in my care was placed back in the Earth north of Santa Fe, New Mexico, as part of the ceremony held for the Return of the Ancestors gathering. The land around Santa Fe had once been ancient Anasazi land. The Anasazi people had been taught by star beings and had ascended to a higher consciousness before they disappeared into the Earth. The first crystal was to be placed in this area to awaken the knowledge of these ancient human beings. I received much information from Mother Spirit before this important crystal ceremony. I was told that this particular area of northern New Mexico would once again become lush and that the wisdom of the divine feminine would flow here before it would in other places. Santa Fe, in particular, would become a focal point for the new consciousness that would be emerging and for the return of the wisdom of the feminine.

I will never forget how, during this ceremony, everyone in the sacred circle (about seventy-five people) became so very quiet and focused as the people channeled all the love in their hearts into this twelve-inch pillar of quartz crystal that I had half-buried in the Earth in the center of the circle. We all focused on loving and healing our blessed Mother Earth, and for at least one hour, we all grounded ourselves between Earth and sky, Great Spirit and Mother Earth, and sent our highest vibration of Love into this potent and ancient crystal. I could see colors—gold and pink or blue—streaming from people's outstretched hands and arms and entering the crystal; I could feel how deeply we all loved our Mother and wept for her, how much we wanted to give back to her and help her become healthy again.

On the third and final day of ceremony, we buried the crystal, full of our prayers and intentions, in a hidden spot away from the circle, sheltered by trees, where it would never be disturbed. As we each filled in the deep hole with handfuls of dirt, we created a kind of natural altar space, every person giving an offering from his or her heart that would remain there, a gift of gratitude and honor to Great Spirit and Mother Earth.

A Crystal for the Redwoods, Our Grand Elders

Several months after the ceremony in Santa Fe, I was contacted by one of the wise indigenous elders on the planet. I was told that the next crystal in my care would need to go to the redwood forests of California, the Grand Elders of planet Earth. These ancient, massive trees are the oldest and wisest of the one-leggeds on our planet, and it is time again for human beings to respect, honor, and protect them. This crystal would help awaken the wisdom they carry and would connect them energetically to other power places on Mother Earth that were now being awakened. It would also serve to restore the sacred feminine on the planet because the feminine wisdom of the heart was now needed to shift human consciousness and heal our way of being on Mother Earth. The redwoods hold a particular frequency for us here on Earth. The spirits of some of our wisest human ancestors have chosen to return in the form of these quiet giants, to guard and watch over us and raise the vibration on Mother Earth. When humanity returns to living from the heart, we will be able to hear and understand this wisdom, to speak with these great spirits.

A small group of six of us from all over the world were being brought together to do this specific ceremony. One of the men was a fellow wisdom keeper whom I had met before. I was the only woman, and the youngest. As the only woman in the group, representing the feminine energy, I would be the one responsible for finding the exact location for the crystal in the forest and for placing the crystal in the ground. I was nervous because this would be only my second crystal ceremony, and I would be traveling by myself in California for a week. I had not really begun to travel yet, so this was a new experience for me. It was intimidating, but I had to put my fears aside and trust that Spirit would guide me.

We all flew to California and met there, to begin several days of prayer and preparation before we could actually do the ceremony. We had specific instructions from our revered elder on what needed to happen. After several days of meditating, praying, singing, and sharing stories, our hearts were in alignment and unified, so we could proceed with the ceremony. The day of the ceremony was very cold, windy, and rainy—somewhat typical for this part of northern California. The day began with a visit to the ocean, where we prayed for guidance to know the exact location for the crystal. Then we progressed to the forest trail. Though we were on public land, we were in an area that was quite secluded and where few tourists came. Something very interesting occurred that morning that none of us expected. We were walking on a small trail, with the ocean to the south of us and the redwood forest to the north of us. I was a bit separated from the group, walking closer to the shoreline. I was clutching my sacred Earth drum and my satchel full of sacred items for ceremony, hoping they would not be soaked through when we found the place.

As I was walking along on the beach, suddenly I heard a crashing sound. A whole herd of elk filed out of the trees and surrounded me, blocking the path into the forest. The bull came within five feet of me and just looked at me. His stance told me that he was somewhere between charging me or allowing me. I realized then that this was his forest and that he would have to allow me to enter it. I stood still, watching his feet and his nostrils, in particular, for signs of his state of being. I began speaking to him through emotion, letting him know that I understood that this was his domain. I asked for permission to enter and explained to him why we were there. He kept his eye on me but then turned his head and began eating some grass. He would allow us to enter the forest. Slowly he turned away and walked back into the forest exactly the way he had come. The other elk stayed where they were and watched our group pass. We entered quietly, with a more profound sense of awe and of the sacredness of what we were there to do.

When we were inside the forest, we walked slowly and reverently among the giants—they were all so beautiful and grand, more magnificent than anything I had ever seen. We were awestruck by the immense presence there. We walked for at least an hour, and I kept my heart as open and receptive as possible, waiting to be given the signal that we had found the right place for the crystal. One could walk for miles and miles in there. I was praying all the while, "Please let me find the right spot." Just when I was starting to worry that I might not find it, I walked up a small hill and heard a voice say clearly, "This is it." I was directed to look at a massive tree trunk before me that stood about ten feet tall and that had been broken off by lightning.

I felt a little uncertain because this tree had died, so I began walking around it. When I got to the back of the tree, there was a large crack that was wide enough to enter. When I slid my body through the crack, I was shocked to find that the tree was hollow inside, like a cathedral. It was at least ten feet in circumference inside this massive redwood trunk. Everyone in our group came inside, and there was still room for more people. I knew without a doubt that this was the spot we were to do ceremony and bury the crystal. We lit candles and placed them in the four directions, and I started drumming my sacred Earth drum. I will never forget the sound it made. It sounded as deep as the Earth herself and vibrated through our bodies and the tree. We began the ceremony and the offering of our prayers.

My eyes welled with tears knowing that this crystal would be buried deep within the body of the tree. After digging the three-foot-deep hole by hand, I held the crystal up. At that moment, amazingly, the sun broke through the clouds and streamed through a crack in the tree, hitting the crystal. Light shot upward. We all felt tingles down our spines. When I dropped the crystal into the hole and it hit the ground with a thud, it felt like the whole tree reverberated. I was then told by Spirit that this location should never be marked or spoken of. No pictures should be taken of the spot, and it was not to be found again—even by the members of our group. You could truly feel the spirits that abounded there.

It's interesting—we always expect something sacred or special to be the biggest or the most beautiful. We assume that the most powerful or best things will be the prettiest to the eye. With our redwood tree, this was not the case. Out of an entire forest of magnificent, healthy trees, the one in which we needed to leave the crystal was one that a person might walk past and overlook entirely, saying, "Oh, this one is dead." Yet this tree trunk now carries within it something immensely powerful, and the energy that vibrates through it will affect every one-legged in the entire area. In fact, it will affect the entire planet and every human being.

Awakening Ancient Lemurian Lands in Hawaii

In the chapter "Return of the Star Beings/Beings of Light," I mention how several kahunas had once appeared in my room to heal me while I was undergoing an energetic rewiring of my body. These ancient medicine men had told me that I would soon be traveling to their lands to open a sacred place there. At the time, I did not realize that these kahunas were from Hawaii, but I remembered this connection when, a month or two after returning from the redwoods in California, my picture screen opened. I was flown over the Earth and taken to one of the smaller Hawaiian islands. I was told that a sacred crystal would need to be placed there to awaken these ancient Lemurian lands and their wisdom. The Lemurians had been a highly advanced civilization that predated Atlantis and that was very much based in the heart. They were deeply feminine and had strong connections with the star beings.

Much about their civilization was truly beautiful. This energy was still present in the Hawaiian people and in these and other Polynesian islands. It was time for this feminine heart energy to awaken once again and assist Mother Earth in her transformation.

At this time, I was shown exactly what crystal I would need to bring to Hawaii, but I did not know where exactly it would need to go or how the whole thing would come about. So I kept this knowledge in my heart and waited. During this time, I had started doing individual healing sessions with people in Santa Fe. One of the people who came to see me was a woman whom I had met before at one of my talks. She lived in Santa Fe part-time and wanted to work with me. About midway through our session, when I was asking for guidance for her, my picture show suddenly opened up. I was told that she was to be the keeper of the crystal that was to be brought to Hawaii—it was to be placed within land of which she currently was the steward. I was told to look for the three stones, the Grandfather, the Grandmother, and the Child, and that this would show me the exact location for the crystal.

When I shared this information with her, I learned that she also lived in Hawaii, on Maui. Several years ago, she had bought some land that she knew in her heart was extremely special, though she wasn't sure why. The place I described matched her land to a tee. Everything was falling into place. With the specifics now more certain, I made plans to fly to Maui a few weeks later, to bring this sacred crystal back home and to awaken the special energies of this ancient Lemurian land.

Having never been to Hawaii, I was amazed by the flowers and fruit trees and the soft, delicately scented air. It struck me as one of the most feminine places on Earth and definitely one of the most beautiful I had ever seen. The land where the ceremony would happen was located on the north shore of Maui, close to Paia. The site had originally been heavily jungled and stretched right down to the sea. There was a freshwater stream on the property that also flowed down to the sea. The day before the ceremony was to happen, I walked the land barefoot, in search of the exact place where the ceremony would need to happen and the crystal would be placed back into the Earth. I was told by Spirit that I should look for three large, ancient, and sacred stones arranged in formation exactly as Orion's Belt. The ancient Hawaiian people had done sacred ceremony there, and those stones were the Grandfather, the Grandmother, and the Child of this land.

I was guided to walk up the hillside into the jungle thicket, full of twisting vines and trees. From there one could gaze out over the Pacific Ocean. Covered under brush and vines, I finally found them—the three large stones. When we cleared them off, they were magnificent. The Grandfather was at least six feet tall, standing erect, with a beautiful plumeria tree growing out of the top. The Grandmother was shaped like a large heart, and the third stone, the Child, sat in the middle of the two giants. The energy coming off the stones was sweet and buzzing with tenderness. I knew I had found the place I was instructed to find. The energy there among these rocks was so intense that it was almost palpable. We began clearing the brush and making the site ready for ceremony the following day.

On this day, something else very unusual, even magical, happened that confirmed for me that this ceremony was going to happen exactly as it was meant to. A few of us were playing games in the grass of the yard, when one of the caretakers of the property strode over to us. "There's a kahuna here outside the gate," he said. "Did you ask him to come?" We all looked at each other. No one had been in touch with a kahuna that we knew of. "He's asking if there's a young blonde woman here." Tingles ran up and down my spine, and I knew something of great importance was about to occur. Very few people knew about the ceremony that was going to take place. I knew in my heart that the native Hawaiian spiritual elders would need to be involved somehow, but I wasn't sure how this was going to happen, even until the day before the ceremony. It wasn't like you just called up the kahunas and invited them. I was worried that the native people might see this ceremony as something done by white outsiders and would not participate at all. As I was about to discover, such was not to be the case.

I walked over to meet this Hawaiian spiritual elder. When he saw me, he took my hands and smiled the kindest smile I have ever seen. He was one of the most gentle, heartfelt, beautiful beings I have ever met. Soon tears were running down his cheeks. He told me something that may sound almost like a fairy tale, but this is how it really happened. He explained that for hundreds of years, there had been a prophecy among his people that a ceremony would happen at this time that would reopen some of the sacred ritual sites. The one who would help to lead the ceremony and bring sacred energies back to the land would come with a gentle rain and be found at the end of a particular rainbow. On this day, he had been eating his lunch when he looked up and saw the special rainbow. He dropped his drink on the floor and got in his car, feeling that the prophecy was playing out. He followed this rainbow to where it ended, which was at the gate of the property. There he waited. That is when he saw the caretaker and asked if there was a young blonde woman there. He welcomed me with an open heart and was very eager for me to accept his apologies—originally he had heard about the ceremony and had doubted its validity. Now he knew that this was a ceremony that his people had prophesied to occur. My heart sang in joy—the native Hawaiian people would participate and colead this ceremony after all!

The morning of ceremony started out with prayers and drumming and watching the sun rise over the ocean. There were only about twelve people present, all of whom had some connection to the land. There was a traditional nose flute player, along with the kahuna and his nephew, a young man who was a gifted singer and who shared sacred chants and stories with us—and who told us about the mythology of this particular place to the Hawaiian people. The ceremony began powerfully, with the kahuna calling to the ancestors and Mother Earth with sacred song. He gave his blessing for the ceremony to begin and offered me gifts from a Lakota brother who had visited the island long ago. He then named me "Little Sister" to the Hawaiian kahunas and blessed me on the "blue road," the Hawaiians' spiritual path, just as Native Americans follow the "red road." He also gave gifts to many of those present.

When it was finally time to place the crystal, we took turns removing the earth and creating a hole to become the crystal's new home. Many tears flowed and hearts opened as we poured our love into the healing of sacred Mother, into the healing of each one of us, and into the raising of the consciousness of the planet. The first person to place the soil over the crystal was a ten-year-old boy, symbolizing the pure, intact masculine, to bless and honor the glorious feminine. He was quiet and a little shy, but what a pure little soul he was.

Next I handed the kahuna a handful of soil with bowed head and bended knee. He placed the soil over the crystal, tears running down his face, then I did the same, with my most heartfelt prayers for beloved Mother; I was followed by the woman who would be the keeper of this crystal. Then everyone else present added his or her handful of soil. With songs and prayers, music and hearts bursting wide open, we closed the ceremony by placing our leis over the sacred spot. This was one of the most magical crystal ceremonies in which I have ever participated. As I walked the land after the ceremony was finished, I kept receiving the words *wahi kapu* over and over. I later learned that this means "sacred place" in native Hawaiian.

Interestingly, about a week after I had returned from Maui, I received a call from an indigenous spiritual elder who had known about the crystal ceremony in Hawaii and who had been keeping tabs on how things went. He told me that I would need to return to the island because something important had not been done. I would need to find the guardian spirit of the place and pay respect to him. According to the elder's instructions, back to Maui I went, to do what was required and complete the ceremony.

The return trip in some ways was just as astounding. I had to locate the bones of the ancient ancestor who had been a protector of the sacred place and offer prayers and respect to him in yet another ceremony. I was guided by Spirit on how to find him. He had been buried standing up within the side of the cliff, gazing out over the sea. To reach this being, I had to descend over the edge of the cliff, high above the sea, being held by my ankles, finally to come face-to-face with a skeleton. Once this guardian spirit had been duly honored, and his acceptance at last obtained, I could finally return home, knowing that the ceremony had been completed and the prophecy fulfilled.

A Crystal to Awaken the "People of the North"

In the chapter "Return of the Star Beings/Beings of Light," I tell of my encounter with an otherworldly being named "Lightning Woman." She had given me very specific information about the "People of the North" and how they would lead the world in remembering who they are. She told me I would soon be journeying to the north and that their hearts and souls were ready to be awakened. These northern countries would become the breadbasket of the world. At the time, I wasn't sure what countries she meant. A few months after this bizarre encounter, I received an invitation to present at a long-running alternative culture and spirituality festival in Sweden called the "No-Mind Festival." Feeling a strong intuition about it, I accepted. I would be there for a week, and the festival would be held in the countryside in a place called "Angsbacka," several hours north of Stockholm.

About a month before I was to leave for Sweden, my picture screen opened, and I was shown that I was supposed to take a particular crystal with me. This would help awaken the ancient wisdom of this land and would serve to awaken the People of the North so that they could fulfill their purpose and lead humanity when the time came. It became clear to me that I was to do a crystal ceremony in Sweden while there—that was the true purpose for me going there. I quickly shifted gears and began working with the organizers because now we would be doing a major ceremony during the festival. The logistics could be challenging. There were already going to be more than a thousand people attending the festival, and we could expect that many would also want to be part of the ceremony, which would be held toward the end of the event.

To this day, the ceremony we did at Angsbacka was the largest public ceremony I have ever done. There were at least eight hundred people present, all arranged in concentric circles in a large field. It was also one of the most powerful ceremonies because of this amplified energy and the sheer number of people focusing their prayers and intentions into the crystal. At the last minute, a Sami woman, of the indigenous people of the region, showed up and blessed the ceremony with a beautiful traditional song. Representing the original people of the land, she placed the crystal in the ground, rekindling the wisdom of her ancient ancestors.

I will never forget how, as people lined up to put their handfuls of soil into the hole to cover the crystal, each person kneeled down, crying and offering his or her heartfelt prayers, some kissing the ground. Men, women, and children all waited their turn—then, when the crystal was buried, something beautiful began to happen. People began to dance and sing and drum, and they danced on the spot where the crystal was, consecrating it with their joyous expression. There was a feeling of unity and pride among the people and an excitement for the future.

I then could truly see why these people would one day lead the world in awakening. Their hearts were so open already, and they were flowing with creativity and spirit. The celebration went on into the evening, and the land itself hummed and buzzed with a new energy.

The Importance of Wearing Quartz Crystal

Because many powerful crystals within Mother Earth are awakening now, and, with them, the ancient knowledge and wisdom with which they were embedded, it is important that we human beings also wear a small piece of quartz crystal at this time. Quartz crystal is one of the most potent conductor crystals. Simply by wearing a small piece of quartz crystal around your neck, you can link yourself to the vast amounts of cosmic energy that are awakening in the master crystals of the Earth. This will affect your energy field; it will help you assimilate these cosmic energies and use them for awakening. I have been asked to share the message that every adult and child should wear a small, clear piece of quartz, if possible. Parents, if children resist or take it off, do not worry. Children are more connected to Earth energy, just as animals are, and their energy fields will more naturally attune themselves. But it will be generally beneficial to all human beings to wear a small piece of clear quartz or to keep a piece with you, as Mother Earth begins to raise her frequency and ancient knowledge begins to awaken on the planet.

Respecting Our Human Treasures

When we speak about the return of the ancient wisdom and living from the heart, it is necessary to look at a few issues in our societies that need to be addressed for us to move forward. Obviously, how we view and treat Mother Earth is the most glaring problem we face; how women and the feminine overall are treated is another problem that needs to be healed. For too long, we have judged as worthless that which is perceived to be vulnerable, soft, feminine, powerless, weak, or dependant. Because "doing" has been so valued over "being," our whole perception of what is valuable and worthy has been skewed. This is most evident in how we in the Western world treat our elders, our children, and our disabled people. When we shift into heart consciousness collectively, we will see that these people are our treasures, our most precious gifts—and that they deserve our respect, love, and protection.

Honoring Our Elders

In many cultures up until our modern times, elders were treated as the wise grandmothers and grandfathers in their communities. They were honored, respected, and taken care of by the entire family in the home. They were fed first, and their word and guidance were paid heed. It was generally acknowledged that they carried within them the wisdom and knowledge of experience and had something vastly valuable to give to their children and grandchildren and to the society as a whole. A person facing old age did not need to be so afraid of becoming decrepit, nonproductive, or a burden on his or her children. The person knew that he or she would have a place, a value, a prestige in the family and community. The elder knew that he or she would be cared for and not left to grow old and die alone. The person knew that he or she would not become invisible or insignificant just by growing old.

Sadly, this is not the case for the elderly in the modern Western world.

It pains me to see how the elderly are treated today. They are often cast away and put somewhere out of sight when they become a burden, or else they themselves choose to live alone until they cannot anymore because they do not want to lose their independence and identity (which is everything in modern Western society) or be a burden to their children. Many adults do not feel responsible for taking care of their elderly parents anymore, and society as a whole does not feel a sense of gratitude or honor toward the elderly. This is a huge spiritual loss because not only do the younger generations not benefit from the wisdom of their elders but those who are growing old (as we all eventually must) do not value themselves. They are robbed of the natural dignity, wisdom, and deepened presence that can otherwise accompany old age. They feel only the diminishment of those things that made them valuable to society such as economic productivity and beauty. This loss is truly tragic for all of us.

Yet it cannot be blamed simply on people not caring for the elderly anymore—it goes much deeper than that. Too many adults in our modern world do not feel responsible for their parents today, often because they felt their parents were not fully responsible and loving to them when they were children. The bonds of familial responsibility and connection seem to have been broken, and this has caused all kinds of wounds and imbalances in our lives and in our societies, and these need fixing.

Nurturing Our Future, the Children

As a society, we also need to value our children. The children truly are our most precious resource and gift. We need to see how much children have to teach us through their pure hearts that are so capable of love and, in turn, to model for them what it means to live in the heart, to be truly loving, steadfast, present, and responsible human beings. We must be aware of what we are teaching them and try our best to be the kinds of human beings we are capable of being, for their sake and the sake of our planet. In fact, the children who are being born today and who are still young at this moment have come to this Earth with huge gifts to share. I have been told, as others have, that these children will lead us when the time comes. They will be the first to start to live from

Love, and they will show us how to do it. Though we adults alive now may be the strongest of the strong souls who will see the dying and rebirth of an entire way of being, the children here now are the purest of the pure and will follow their hearts and lead us all in living a totally new way. If we knew the treasures with which we have been entrusted, we would make sure that every child receives what he or she needs to grow into health and wholeness; it should matter not that "this is my child" and "that is your child"—as societies and communities, we need to take responsibility for guarding, protecting, and nurturing every child into his or her fullness. We must rise into what we are capable of and become the beings we were meant to become. We must remember who we are—we are not wounded, limited, flawed, sinful, and helpless. We are co-creators and have the divine Love that created us within us. We can and must change how we treat the children and, in that, rebirth ourselves.

The Beauty of the Different

There is one other group of beings among us who have been grossly neglected and devalued for centuries. Our disabled people play a very special role in this Earth life, if we could but truly see them—and yet they have often been thrown away, ignored, abused, or treated with fear and disdain within our families and communities. Our mentally and physically disabled often chose to come here to hold a very high frequency on this planet. As many of us know, those who were born mentally disabled are often the purest, most angelic souls. Their energy vibrates ten times that of other human beings. They are incapable of ego, malice, or hate. They have an innocence that, if we would open to it and see its beauty, would cause us to remember how to love and have gratitude for life.

Spirit has shown me that many of our disabled people are actually light beings who have come here to hold a high frequency that is helping human beings to evolve. They chose the one place where they would never have to worry about being detected, the one place we would never look for them. Yet these beings, disguised as our disabled, are serving the planet in ways we can never imagine. The next time you encounter a disabled person, do not walk past him or her, averting your eyes; rather, give the person a smile and a hello, for he or she is a truly magnificent souls who is hiding in a form that we humans overlook and disdain. The disabled are not here to teach—they are here simply to hold a vibration of love so that we do not destroy ourselves and our planet, so that we keep moving forward. Just as the whales and dolphins are here from elsewhere in the cosmos, holding a high vibration for the planet, so are our mentally disabled.

I have had the honor of growing up among siblings who are mentally disabled. To this day, I count as one of my greatest gifts that I got to be the sister of the pure, angelic beings who are my brothers. I have no words to describe my love for them and what they have taught me about love, about beauty, about purity of heart—and what they are still teaching me. I wish for them a new world in which they will never be judged or scorned again, in which the hearts of human beings overflow with love and tenderness for all our most precious human treasures—our elders, our children, and our disabled.

Letting Go of Judgment

If this Earth life truly is a journey of learning and growth, and we are all here to learn different lessons and have different experiences given to us by our higher selves, then how can we judge ourselves or others? If you are perfect as you are and I recognize you as God or Goddess, then I have no right to judge you or the path you are taking. If we wanted to be perfect beings, we would not have come here and inherited a human body that is tender and breakable and a heart that is complicated and vulnerable. We wouldn't have come to a place where we could make such vast mistakes. Yet our mistakes are exactly how we learn here and, in fact, are not mistakes at all. There is no such thing as a mistake to the soul, only a learning opportunity.

We make mistakes and do things that make us angry at ourselves. We say, "I wish I wouldn't have done that" and feel ugly, thinking we have failed or that we are weak, worthless, and flawed. We are so very hard on ourselves. Most of us can understand the moral idea that it is not right to judge others and try not to be too judgmental, but when it comes to ourselves, we have a field day. Most of the time, we never even notice how harshly we are judging ourselves.

When we judge ourselves, we cause our light to diminish; we put a dusty cloak over our light. We forget that we are sparks of divine Love and that our higher selves have come to this Earth to learn certain lessons. We are perfect just as we are, experiencing what we are meant to experience—including the mistakes and challenges and so-called failures. In getting caught up in judgment, we forget who we really are and what we are capable of. We are gods and goddesses, if we could truly see ourselves from a universal perspective. Everything is in divine order. When we judge ourselves or others, we feel separate from our divinity, small and helpless.

Sometimes those of us who are more consciously spiritual judge other people who are not consciously spiritual or looking for deeper meaning in life. This is not really that different from a religious person judging another person who has not "seen the light of truth" and who is therefore fallen or sinful. It's so easy to do this unconsciously—to think we are right and have found the way that everyone should follow. But when we really understand that each person is here on his or her own learning journey and has a Great I AM, that each person is perfect as he or she is, we can start to free ourselves from judgment. I can let my neighbor be who she is without trying to change her. I can start to love her because she is perfect as she is, a divine spark just as I am, learning what her higher self sent her here to learn. We are all here learning different lessons for our growth and evolution, and in this sense, no one lesson is higher or lower, more spiritual or less spiritual, than another.

The one thing that loves you more than anything in the universe is your own higher self. Instead of blaming yourself, God, or the universe for what happens to you, for the particular lessons you have needed to learn and the hardships you have had to undergo, you can remember that your own higher self is guiding you with love and providing exactly the experiences and opportunities you need to learn and grow here. Instead of feeling like a victim or feeling self-judgment or self-pity, you can know that your own higher self is in charge, guiding you through life with infinite compassion and wisdom.

Letting others be who they are without judging them also means that I, too, can let go of worrying about what others think of me. A wise elder once gave me a piece of advice of which I remind myself every day. He said, "What others think of you is none of your business." Whether they think highly of me or lowly of me, I do not have to get caught up in their opinions or let their perceptions affect my energy. When we are being thought of highly, we never notice how we are buying in to others' projections, yet when others are projecting negativity on us, and do not like us, we can see how dependent we are on what others think of us and how easily we can let ourselves be discouraged from our path. There is an enormous loss of power when we start believing and giving energy to what others say or think about us.

Since I started doing public work and speaking, I have had to contend with others' projections on me, both positive and negative. With great gifts always come great challenges. It was something I have had to struggle with inwardly—and when it first started happening and I realized that I could no longer hide or recede back into anonymity, I had to dig deep into my soul and make a decision. Would I stand true to my path and my soul's calling? Would I bend or break in the face of opposition, ridicule, or criticism? Did I believe in myself enough not to let others' approval or disapproval affect me? It is easy to think that those out there in public roles are not as vulnerable or sensitive to criticism and negativity, but they are often more so. Through this extremely challenging process, I was able finally to say yes, I will do what I came to this planet to do, despite whatever negativity comes at me, whether people like me and support me and my message or criticize and ridicule me. Sometimes we need to find our inner Warriors, to root ourselves in our deepest authenticity, and to fully surrender to Spirit come what may if we want to fulfill our souls' purposes here. As those of you who have stepped forward in any kind of public or visible role know, it takes tremendous courage to step out and be visible, to step into your true power—to fulfill your heart's calling, regardless of what others think of you.

The issue of judging ourselves and others is so important because it affects our energy and how much we are able to love. It affects how we feel and how we see. We are being taught that the time has come to stop using our eyes and minds only to judge things and to start using our hearts. Our eyes and minds are always discriminating and making surface judgments about things, whether they are good or bad, beautiful or ugly. I have had to learn lessons about this myself—Spirit has shown me specific times when I took the surface appearance for reality and missed an important teaching that was trying to come to me.

Letting go of judgment is not just an individual task but a collective task for humanity. It has always seemed absurd to me how human beings have judged (and discriminated against) other human beings historically for things like the color of their skin, what religion they follow, their ethnicity, or whom they love. Although some of these forms of judgment are now recognized by our society as discrimination and therefore as wrong and unjust, some are still widely accepted and practiced. This is the case with the treatment of gays and lesbians, at least in American society, as this is being written. Judging a person because of whom he or she loves, male or female, is the most ridiculous thing to me. In the future, we will see the discrimination in this area and the lack of human rights for gays and lesbians as inhumane and backward, just as racial segregation is now widely seen as inhumane and backward. Love is the one thing that can save this planet and is the most profound thing in existence. If we are to awaken as humanity, we will need to expand vastly how we think of love and the human heart and stop oppressing and condemning those who are different from us.

To move into the space of the heart and to change our collective future, we must let go of the tendency to judge ourselves and others and open to the perfection and freedom that exist within us as our own higher selves.

PART III
Visions of the Present and the Future

Spirit Guides, Teachers, and Communications through the Picture Screen

As I have mentioned throughout the book, I often receive information through particular spirit guides who appear to me and teach me or who have a message to share. My primary spirit guide thus far has been a being called "Mother Spirit." She has told me that she is the "mother of all children," including the plants and animals, and that her soul runs through all our veins. She is less than five feet tall and looks to be about sixty years old and of indigenous South American heritage. She is bare chested with red clay–like paint down her chest and belly and wears a natural fiber covering around her hips. Her hair is silky black and cut straight across her forehead in a bowl shape, with yellow, orange, and red feathers in the back that appear to be from birds-of-paradise or another tropical bird. There are two stripes across her forehead, one blue, the other red, and she wears yellow woven armbands. In addition to Mother Spirit, I have been taught by spirit guides and beings from several indigenous traditions as well as by beings whom I cannot place but whom I assume to be ascended Masters. Sometimes I am spoken to in words and can transcribe what I am receiving, but other times, I receive a direct spiritual transmission that is beyond words. My instructions, or the messages I am given, are often quite specific.

The Picture Show

The other way in which I am taught and given information is through a kind of inner screen that opens up in my vision. I call it my "picture show." I see and watch things on this screen, which opens up quite unexpectedly. I am often taken on a kind of interdimensional journey and shown various places on Earth, images, symbols, and sometimes highly esoteric information. I am transported to different places on Earth and shown different things, in clear detail. In these chapters, I share much of the information I have been shown through this inner screen. I do not pretend to understand all of what I have been shown or why exactly I have been shown it, but I share it with you, assuming that it is important and that its meaning will be revealed to me and to all of us collectively at some point in the near future.

At first, when the screen appears, I will often see many strange, disparate images that change every few seconds, almost like a television channel being flipped. Sometimes I will see images that clearly do not belong to this planet, places we could not imagine existing. Then the images will settle into one particular channel, and whatever I am supposed to be shown or taught will begin. I not only see things through this screen but can experience them directly, with my senses. I can speak to someone and interact. For example, I once met with a very wise old man who seemed to live somewhere in Mongolia. I was taken into his family dwelling, offered food, and shown his surroundings in detail. I still remember his crinkled face and kind smile, the smell of the food his wife cooked, and the look of his clothes. He taught me about the importance of having a pure heart, taught it through his very being when we connected through the heart.

I have also met with a group of men who all wore white and who called themselves the "Mamos"—only later did I learn that these are the priests of the Kogi tribe living high in the mountains of Columbia, some of the most spiritually advanced beings on the planet. I remember them as some of the most loving beings I have ever encountered, with a real playfulness and sense of humor that they were eager to share with me. When I saw a picture of these Kogi Mamos in a book I was reading, I was shocked to see men who looked exactly like those I had met through my picture screen.

Opening the Picture Screen

I was taught that this picture screen, through which I am given lessons and shown information, is the "Universal One Mind–One Love–One Light–One Energy." Though I am not sure exactly what makes this screen appear, there is a meditation that I use that will often open this screen to me. First, I breathe energy up from Mother Earth through the soles of my feet. I breathe it up through my body and release it through the top of my head, sending it up to the heavens. Then I breathe energy down from Great Spirit through the top of my head, down through my body, and send it deep into the Earth. In this way, you can anchor to both Mother Earth and Great Spirit. When I feel a sense of euphoria, a blissful feeling coursing throughout my body, I begin doing this on each inhalation and exhalation. On each inhalation, I send Mother Earth energy up through me to the cosmos. On each exhalation, I breathe down cosmic energy from Great Spirit, sending it deep into the Earth. Doing this creates a feeling of spaciousness and bliss. The picture show will often start when I am anchored in this state.

Wisdom Keepers

I have also been taught by flesh-and-blood, living teachers and have received much guidance and information from spiritual elders and other wisdom keepers. When I became shaman, I was told by the elder who guided my initiation and by Mother Spirit that I was one of twelve wisdom keepers who were on the planet at the time, all receiving similar information about the changes coming to Mother Earth, and all with a specific purpose. When people ask me specifics about who the other wisdom keepers are, I can only say that they are real human beings who, for the most part, know who they are. Some are indigenous, some are not. I have met several of them in person and have spoken on the telephone to others, but I do not necessarily know all of them or their everyday names and where they come from. We are always introduced to each other through our spirit names. It may seem far-fetched, but there is no secretary, leader, or planner of these meetings—many times, we all receive inner guidance on where and how to meet, and somehow a meeting happens, whether in person, by telephone, or through the picture screen.

I cannot say who these people are publicly because it is for them to decide whether to be known. Some of them are operating under the radar and do not wish to be known or recognized in their real spiritual capacity, or they require anonymity to do their work. Even speaking about this is difficult because the rational human mind wants proof and logical evidence, a paper trail and membership roster, and what I am describing is something not bounded by space and time and dimensionality—but that is nonetheless very real.

I want to make it clear that there are many highly evolved spiritual beings on this planet who are keeping the vibration high and fulfilling important spiritual tasks. This particular group of individuals is connected through a shared spiritual mission and through the specific information we are responsible for receiving and sharing. In a general sense, there are many wise beings who might be called "wisdom keepers" on the planet right now, but when I use this term, I am referring specifically to the group of individuals of which I am a part, who receive similar information from Spirit and who share a common cosmic purpose at this time, each fulfilling different roles and tasks. I use this term because it was given to me directly from Spirit, as it was given to the others.

In December 2009, I was called to take part in an impromptu meeting (via telephone) of several wisdom keepers, along with an important spiritual elder. We had spoken before on the telephone as well as through the picture screen to share information and visions we had been receiving. The meeting was called to discuss the recent appearance of the "blue star" over various parts of the world. During these meetings, in which I participated, those present shared their visions and information they were receiving spiritually, including specific guidance that was being received by some of our spiritual elders. Most often, the information we were receiving was the same, though sometimes a particular person was given some piece that others were not.

During this meeting, we discussed that the blue star had been sighted in Colorado, Utah, Greece, and Norway. Our spiritual elder told us that actually, it was not a star but a higher frequency of energy, a massive energy portal for star beings. This so-called blue star had been prophesied to appear by many indigenous peoples, including the Hopi, before the Earth would go through her heavenly change. This energy coming with the blue star would assist humanity in its eventual ascension to the fifth dimension of Love. We were told to listen with our hearts because these energies were here now in our fields.

This energy portal was now open, and through it, star beings were coming to specific locations on Earth, where they had lived before. These special, sacred places on Earth included Pumapunku in Bolivia, the ancient stone circles of Europe, the Native American lands and deserts of North America, Solomon's Temple in the Holy Land, Giza in Egypt, a particular ancient area in Greece, and the pyramids in South America. The star beings helped in building these places and had once dwelt there; now they were returning to help bring sacred truths back and to help humans bring forth truths that have been buried.

We were told that star beings will once again work side by side with human beings; just by their presence, they will raise our vibration. There is nothing to do but just to be. We human beings can change the course of our history. The number of us remembering the power of Love is changing the future. We are further along than the ancient ones thought. Our choices can change the future. Because of this, we may not need to be shaken to our core during the great change. The more our hearts grow, the less destruction we may need to experience. Our day-to-day acts of kindness help Earth ascend to her heavenly state. We are being told to be Love and to let Love be our religion. This is what all the truly great masters have taught: Love. There is nothing to do except just to be Love.

After the meeting was finished, I found myself pondering all that had been said: could it really be this simple? Could we really change the future of our world by being more loving and kind? This was the message I had been receiving, over and over, from the other side since I had become Little Grandmother. I knew that this message was exactly what I would need to speak on and to share with the children of Earth. It was urgent, because we still had time to affect the outcome of events likely to change our world.

Teachers from the Stars

I will always remember another very unusual meeting of wisdom keepers to which I was urgently summoned. This was to be a meeting in the flesh. In fact, I was told to drop everything and go! I was in Colorado at the time, running errands. My children were at school. I was driving in my car when, all of a sudden, my picture screen began to open. I pulled over so I could focus on what was happening. The message cried, "Wisdom keepers—go now!" It directed us to a particular place I was shown on a map. It was in New Mexico, close to Taos. I was even being shown the route and directions on how to get there to find the specific building. I had never received such an urgent message through my picture screen. I started scrambling and making calls to try to arrange to have my kids picked up from school. My mind was racing trying to think of what I should bring and what the purpose of the meeting could be.

A half hour later, I was on the road, headed south toward Taos, about an hour and a half drive. While driving, I had to completely give over to the picture show, which was showing me where to turn. This is not an easy task, to be open to one's inner vision while driving. So much was going through my mind. Would I find the right place? If I found the right place, would others be there? Should I have brought more with me than just my little briefcase filled with my most precious crystals, medicine bag, and sage?

At this point, I had only met most of the other wisdom keepers through the picture screen or on the telephone, not face-to-face. Would I meet them now in person? All I knew was that I was being asked to go *now* to this unknown place in the middle of the high desert, and it was extremely important.

I made the turn at the stop sign I had previously seen on my picture screen and headed south toward New Mexico. Before reaching the town, I was told to turn off. As I was driving down a remote road, it looked like nothing at all would be out there, but soon a small building with several cars parked outside appeared. I slowly pulled in and took a deep breath. When I walked up to the door and opened it, I saw a small group of people sitting around in chairs in a circle, with one seat still open. Everyone smiled and welcomed me, knowing who I was already. I recognized only two people, wisdom keepers I had seen on my screen; the rest were completely new to me, including one large man standing at the edge of the circle. This man was well over six and a half feet tall and very pale white with a blonde, almost white, hair color. He was very welcoming, and his smile was so perfectly full of love that instantly, I felt at home.

I should tell you right now that this was no ordinary man. His eyes were most incredible, and I couldn't take my eyes off him. Instead of having a white part of the eye, a colored iris, and a pupil, as we humans do, this man's eyes were entirely black. He was the most beautiful man I had ever seen; pure beauty and love emanated from his whole being, though he was clearly not human.

Now that we were all together, we could begin. He spoke first of the coming age on planet Earth and how many life-forms, including his people, who were from the star of Sirius, are watching us at all times. He explained that human beings are going through a pivotal shift that almost all life-forms go through but that there was something very unique about us. We are evolving and changing at a supersonic pace that has never been seen before in the cosmos. We human beings are going through an evolution of consciousness and making progressive leaps, much faster than any life-form before. For this reason, we had caught the attention of the other beings in our galaxy and other galaxies. He explained that planet Earth is like a child in its spiritual evolution compared to other places, and yet we are growing and making giant leaps in consciousness because of our special placement in the solar system. Great bursts of energy from the Sun are helping us speed up and raise our consciousness at a pace never seen before.

He spoke to us like we were children, most beloved children, and told us how other life-forms love us a great deal and want us to succeed in going forward. Planet Earth would be going through this shift with or without us. With tenderness and kindness, he expressed how those of us on Earth at this time were a very special people, very strong souls pulled by a deep yearning to be in alignment with universal Truth and Love. He said that we humans, as a species, are getting closer to a dramatic leap in consciousness but that the only thing holding us back is our egotistic way of being. He spoke of how Love is the universal energy that creates all things and that it is time for humanity to remember this—to fully love ourselves as great beings—and that through this remembrance, we can achieve a way of being that is almost too great to imagine.

He then showed us on a screen, much like the window that opens up for me, an image of the Earth. There were dots of light in various places all over the planet; the rest was blackness. These points of light are the souls living today whose hearts are in alignment, those who have raised their frequency and are living in the heart. Although their numbers are still small, they are enough to give hope to planet Earth and her children. He expressed with urgency how we must teach other human beings how to live from the heart, to remember the love we come from and how splendid we are, to multiply these lights. As we grow in numbers in love, we can change our universal consciousness from mind and ego to Love—and when that happens, the world will change because we truly are the creators of our experience and can change the course of our planet. It is of greatest importance now.

When he was done speaking, he had each one of us share what information we had each been receiving in our own special ways, what we were teaching the people, how we were trying to make a difference. One man spoke about being a communicator between different indigenous peoples, connecting them and helping them share their prophecies and teachings. One woman who was a sound healer spoke about how her role was to illuminate the power of sound, frequency, and light for our planet. Another man was in constant communication with beings from Sirius and was communicating to human beings what their role is in helping humanity. One of the wisdom keepers whom I had recognized was working with beings from the "inner Earth." When it was my turn, I spoke about the calling I had received to gather together the "tribe of many colors." This coming together was essential for increasing the numbers of those living in their hearts, raising the vibration on the planet.

Each and every one of us had a turn to speak to the group, and then the man spoke to us individually, answering our questions and addressing our doubts and fears. When he came to me, I expressed how I had been feeling worried about failing, about what others would think of me, and was afraid of being criticized. He asked me, "At the end of your days, when you reflect on your life, can you accept that you didn't fulfill your purpose because you cared about the opinions of others?" He stressed that it was imperative for me and for all of us to see the big picture, to see the importance of why we were here and what we had come to do.

After speaking to each of us personally, he gave us a small blessing and then walked out of the room. We all took our time to speak to each other about all we had heard and experienced. It was clear to all of us why we were summoned to this meeting with such urgency. Humanity was now within a small window of time before the Earth changes that had already started would be complete. New energies had just begun pouring down to our planet from the heavens, to help as many people as possible shift their consciousness and start living from a higher vibration. What we did now as a human species was crucial. Would we as human beings go forward with Mother Earth into a higher frequency, or would we be removed from Earth? Would those of us who could tune in to higher frequencies and communicate with the light beings follow our hearts and fulfill the pledges we had made in coming here to planet Earth?

We left the meeting with renewed passion and commitment to follow our individual callings and to do so in full force, without holding back. This new energy coming to Earth would assist us in doing our work, and for all beings that could open to it, amazing leaps of consciousness were now possible. The cosmos was doing all it could to help us, and many loving and highly advanced beings were now with us, watching us, holding their breath to see what we would do next.

Return of the Star Beings/
Beings of Light

Although our culture still treats discussion of other life-forms in the cosmos with skepticism and ridicule, more and more of us are wanting a more open-minded and reasonable discussion of the issue of other life in the universe. Because of how the subject is treated in the media, I, too, was always wary of talk of ETs, aliens, or UFOs for most of my life. Yet ironically, I had firsthand evidence that there were other beings out there. I was one of those people who had seen unexplained lights over the house in the area where I grew up, a hot spot for UFO phenomena. I had also had several encounters with beings that I could only describe as not of this world. Yet I did not speak about them, as many people did not, for fear of sounding crazy. I still worry about being pegged as the shaman who talks about aliens and put in a certain new age box. The time has now come to speak of what I have seen and been shown about our brothers and sisters from the stars.

Since I became Little Grandmother, I have been shown clearly by Spirit that the time for such denials of other life in the universe is about to be over. Humanity is very close to remembering that we do indeed have "brothers and sisters from the stars." The governments of the Earth have started loosening the tight noose of secrecy around the knowledge of extraterrestrial life. There have already been partial disclosures by governments and government officials and an opening of classified UFO files to the public. Soon there will be a full disclosure of the level to which other life-forms have been interacting with humanity from the beginning, and when this happens, our notions of religion and where we all come from will radically alter. For those of you who already believe in star beings, or have experienced them, this will come as no surprise. To more traditionally minded or skeptical readers, I offer you what I have personally experienced and been taught about these star beings so that you can weigh it with your hearts and minds and decide for yourself.

In late September 2010, a landmark press conference was held at the National Press Club in Washington, D.C., that was covered by CNN and national news media, where ex–military officers and high-ranking officials discussed their experiences with UFOs during their service. As of this writing, you can watch the entire video of this remarkable press conference on YouTube. One of the speakers, a retired air force officer, described how he and his team had witnessed UFOs hovering over nuclear missiles and even disabled them. This was also reported by others charged with keeping watch over these sensitive areas of national security. When I heard these disclosures, I was amazed that the government had not undertaken an immediate investigation and that this information had somehow never made it to the public. One would think that UFOs disabling our nuclear missiles would be a top story—and would require some serious national attention! But even more than this, it confirmed what I already knew to be true about the star beings—that they are actually here for a benevolent purpose and are even helping to protect us from ourselves.

What exactly do I mean when I use the term *star being*? This is the term Spirit uses when I am taught about our "brothers and sisters from the stars." I try not to use the more conventional term *extraterrestrial* because I think it has some skewed popular connotations. This term makes us think of beings we have seen in Hollywood movies such as *E.T. the Extra-Terrestrial* and *Close Encounters of the Third Kind*—and also makes them seem very solid and three-dimensional, like us. What I have experienced of these beings, or at least one or two species of them, is that they are more made of light than solid matter. Sometimes I will use the term *being of light* to describe them because this feels more accurate. This term has a very different feel to it and makes one think of angels more than aliens; it takes into account that these beings operate at higher dimensions of consciousness—not just that they are from another planet or star. I have not experienced personally the forms of life that some refer to as grays, reptilians, or more stereotypically alien-looking beings; rather, those I have experienced seemed to shimmer with luminosity and were in fact humanoid looking, though larger. These beings seemed to glide more than walk, and when they spoke, it was more like music or a sound vibration than words that humans use. In this sense, they were light beings, though I know they do indeed originate from elsewhere in the cosmos.

I have learned that all beings, all life-forms, are created by the same universal consciousness and Love that created human beings. In one important way, the star beings are like us—they, too, can grow, evolve, and become more advanced in their consciousness. I have seen that for most of these beings, the laws of free will and spiritual accountability still operate. The star beings with whom I have been in contact have not told me specifically where they come from, with a name or location on the galactic map, yet they were clearly of the highest vibration of love and kindness. They were very concerned for human beings, much like an older brother or sister or parent would be concerned for a child. But clearly not all the beings out there are like this. I have been shown that in the past, there have been beings who have been motivated by self-interest, greed, and power (much like human beings!) and who have visited this planet mainly to take resources and to study how we breathe, live, and reproduce, for their own ends.

I have been told by Spirit that there is a race of beings from a planet called "Planet X" or "Nibiru" that had great interest in Earth for her physical resources and who had been coming here to take them. Their planet suffered from having had no sunlight for years on end and hosted an overpopulation of beings with dwindling resources. They had been coming here and doing harm, but the star beings of the highest vibration came together to put an end to this abusive intrusion. Although these things are scary, and we may be tempted to say that certain star beings are therefore evil, they are really acting in the same way humans might if their survival were threatened. They, too, were trying to save themselves and their children from extinction. Yet these beings were of a lower vibration than many others in the cosmos and posed a threat to human beings and the Earth.

I was told by those star beings that love us like parents and who have high hopes for us that these intrusive visitations by certain species were stopped in the year 2000. These benevolent star beings intervened on our behalf, and it was found that certain cosmic laws were being violated by these harmful interactions. There are in fact great interplanetary councils and federations that spiritually govern the galaxies, made up of beings from various star nations (*Star Trek* was not totally far-fetched!).

Our Ancient Forebears and Teachers

During the ceremony we held in 2009 for the Return of the Ancestors gathering, one important aspect of ceremony was to invite our ancient ancestors and their wisdom back into our lives, to honor them and welcome their return. Though one dimension of this had to do with the generations of human beings who had come before us, it also had another, more esoteric meaning: it related to the star beings, those even more ancient forebears who actually helped human civilization and imparted to us great knowledge and wisdom, long before recorded human history. Spirit has shown me that beings from other places in the universe have actually created, or helped to create, many of the most ancient and sacred temples and pyramids using spiritual technologies that humanity has long since forgotten or never possessed itself.

I have been shown that the pyramids in Egypt, for example, and, in particular, the Sphinx, predate humanity and that there is in fact a great library of information beneath the right paw of the Sphinx that would clearly reveal our connection to the star beings and their spiritual knowledge and technologies. Whether this exists in three-dimensional form or needs to be accessed via a higher frequency of consciousness, I am not certain. I have also been shown that there are pyramids on the Moon that exactly mirror the pyramids of Giza, Egypt, and Tikal, Guatemala. These were not made by human hands. The purpose of these pyramids is very far from scientists' understanding of them as tombs—they were actually used as conductors of sound or frequency and acted as portals to the cosmos and higher dimensions of reality. Although I can offer no proof of this other than what I have been shown, I know that what I have seen corresponds with information many other seers and wisdom keepers have esoterically received and experienced.

In addition, I was recently shown in a teaching through my picture screen that there are ancient cities within the Earth with portals in South America, the Arctic, and Spain, where ancient indigenous peoples still live to this day. There are actually very evolved human beings living within our planet who were taught how to use crystals for light and other ancient, galactic tools to live within Mother Earth. They grow crops, have running water, have a powerful light and energy source, and, to this day, still work and live side by side with star beings. When I was shown this, I was told that this knowledge would be coming out to the public in the year 2011, as would other great and life-changing truths that we can now only imagine. (Please see the chapter "The Uncovering of Ancient Truths and Wisdom" for more about this.)

When I was in Hawaii to do a crystal ceremony on Maui, I had to locate the exact place where the crystal was to be placed, in an area that had been recognized as sacred in the distant past by the Hawaiians. When I was walking the land, determining where the spot might be, I received guidance from Spirit that I was to find three large stones that mirrored Orion's Belt: Grandmother, Grandfather, and the Child. The crystal would need to be placed among these stones. I was told that these stones were not placed by human beings. Imagine my joy and surprise when I did in fact find these three massive boulders, covered in overgrowth and moss, set exactly as the three stars of Orion's Belt. Such ancient and profound energy emanated from them, each quite different from the other. These stones connected to that place in the cosmos from which those who placed them came. The ancient Hawaiians, I was told, were descendants of the Lemurians, an ancient and beautiful civilization that had much knowledge from and connection with star beings. After receiving information such as this very often, I have come to understand that beings from other places in the cosmos and other dimensions have been interacting with humanity for a very long time, have seeded spiritual knowledge and technologies that have shaped human civilization—and that very soon, our collective amnesia about this will be removed!

Spotlight on Planet Earth

There is so much interest in planet Earth and human beings among all life in the universe. Earth is beautifully situated in our galaxy to receive ample light from the sun, nurturing so many amazing life-forms, and the consciousness of human beings has been able to make extraordinary leaps. Our advancement in spiritual maturity is being watched by many beings. We are close to making the largest leap ever on an evolutionary scale, whereby we will be able to join our brothers and sisters of the cosmos in operating on the higher frequencies of light. We will once again know that we are just one part of a whole cosmos of beings—our isolation and amnesia, our feeling of separation from our divine or celestial home, from God, will be no more. We will know that we are gods and goddesses and will rediscover all our latent potential and faculties. We will use all of our brains, not just a small percentage, as we have been. This will open reality to us in a way we cannot imagine. We will make an evolutionary leap. It is no exaggeration to say that in the future, we will communicate with people across the world, and we will not need the Internet or telephones to do so.

We are one of the youngest planets and species in the cosmos. Compared to other races of beings, we truly are like infants in our capacities and spiritual understanding. Yet it is no exaggeration to say that we are so very loved, and Mother Earth herself is regarded as a most precious, exquisite being of incomparable beauty by many star beings. I have been told that among all the millions of places we might choose to be born, planet Earth is one of the hardest, and yet it is also the greatest gift. Not everyone gets to come here. It is a kind of graduate school for souls. Experiencing physicality and having this human body is more precious than we can ever know. We were not meant to be perfect and to sit in meditation all day in a cave, transcending this human body—we came here to experience duality and the entire complex mixture of emotions and experiences that make us human. This is precisely what makes us so interesting to all the other beings in the universe, many of whom do not have our range of emotions or our distinct physicality, along with our vast spiritual capacities into which we have barely tapped.

The extremely evolved star beings who have been present on Earth since the very beginning of human life are even now watching over us and are keenly interested in our progress, just like parents would watch over their children. What I am about to say may seem outlandish, or may offend those with a religious view of creation, but I have been told that these beings helped to create human beings. They seeded the human race on planet Earth. If this seems far too sci-fi or fantastical, consider how we have been taught by religion that we were created from a grain of sand, or even a rib! The idea that we evolved from apes or that we originated from a single cell in the ocean requires huge leaps of imagination, and even faith. Is it so hard to believe that beings of a loving and much higher intelligence might have created human beings? Even we human beings (who are at the low end of the totem pole in terms of our advancement among beings) have figured out how to clone animals, genetically engineer fruits and vegetables, and many other things soon to be revealed. It's not actually that far-fetched. If star beings helped to create the human race, this does not mean that there is no Creator or original spiritual power governing the entire enterprise. But it does dramatically change our perception of who we are, where we come from, and what we are capable of achieving.

Meetings with Star Beings

My first encounter with a being of light is described in the chapter "All Things Are Alive with Energy." One night, as I was camping in the wilderness, I was visited by a being of light—a shimmering form of a woman who was not made of flesh and blood but who appeared to be made of small pixels of closely clustered blue specks of light. She spoke to me in the form of music, and when I awoke, I was able to see dots of color and energy in everything alive. This encounter was different from my encounters with spirits or spirit guides. She was not a spirit of a human being or ancestor now passed but some sort of celestial being, from another place or dimension. At a certain point, it becomes hard, with our limited human consciousness, to make the distinction between a spirit and a being from another dimension or place in the galaxy. Clearly our understanding of multidimensionality and consciousness is still in its infant stages.

Since that night, I have communicated with beings of light several times, never when I ask them to come or when I want to speak to them but rather when they need to speak with me. Their appearance is always accompanied by the sensation of warm water being poured from my head to my toes. Sometimes they have a message for me. To me, these beings seem to be made of light and are most gentle and loving.

The other kind of star being I have encountered was different in that it was seemingly more solid and quite human looking. These beings have all been males and looked very much alike to my eyes. They are about seven feet tall, and their skin is very fair, with hair so blonde that it is almost white. The most intriguing thing about them is their manner of moving. They do everything very gently and elegantly, without that strange clumsiness human beings have because of gravity, feeling the weight of our bodies as we move. The way they walk reminds me of walking on a moving walkway because they seem to glide with very fast, long strides, almost as if they are walking on air. I describe meeting one such being in the chapter "Spirit Guides, Teachers, and Communications through the Inner Screen." Both times I have spoken with these beings, they spoke entirely about their love for the human race.

One evening, I had such an encounter. I was in my yard in Colorado, sitting out by the pond, meditating. I was paying attention to the energy of the rosebush in front of me when, all of a sudden, three beings appeared before me. They were male and looked as I have described. One began speaking to me. He told me how much they love human beings, the children of Mother Earth. He explained how blessed we were in the eyes of all that lived and how we have caught the attention of all beings because we are leaping into higher levels of consciousness faster than any beings ever have before. He also spoke for a long while about how human beings were created in love, as an act of love by other star beings long ago who were highly advanced in love and the laws of the universe and creation.

One thing he said has stuck with me very strongly. He said that we were loved by these wondrous beings "ten thousand times as strongly as a human mother could love her child." At this point, his eyes welled up with tears. I sat transfixed as he spoke about how heartbreaking it is to them that we humans are so afraid of them. Speaking softly and slowly, he asked me to think about my children and what it would feel like if I, their mother, were to walk into their room and they were terrified of me, if I were to go to them to try to console them and only made them more frightened because they didn't understand and couldn't calm down enough to listen. My heart understood why he was asking this of me, and I, too, started to cry.

He explained that until we open our hearts, until we get to a place where we will not strike out in fear, they cannot come to us, even though

they want to. They cannot come to teach us until we are no longer terrified of them. I saw the love in his eyes as he spoke of the deep mis-
understanding we have of them, of how we have been taught nothing
about them and how their existence has been lost to our memory. We
have believed in ideas that have led us to live in fear, to not be able to
perceive certain things. Until we ask them to come back, they will not.

They are willing to teach us what they know, to help us in taking
better care of the Earth and each other, but we have to ask. They will
not interfere and save us. We must learn and grow and clean up our
own mess. If they were to solve our problems for us, we would not grow
or evolve as we are intended. They will return, but only when we have
shifted enough so that we will not strike out in fear and cause further
destruction, when we have opened our hearts to them and to a larger
perspective of reality. They are waiting to assist us, but we must reach
a higher vibration at which we are able to perceive and communicate
with them. This is what I mean when I say they have always been here.
Most of the time, human beings are not experiencing reality in a high
enough state of consciousness to be able to attune to the frequency in
which they exist. When we open our hearts and start living from Love
consciousness, we will open up access to communicate with beings
who exist in dimensions beyond our three-dimensional material reality.

Another powerful experience I have had with a star being still leaves
me in wonder to this day. The day before the encounter, I had seen a
white light in the sky that had grown larger and then disappeared. Soon
after, I felt a strong tingling sensation in my chest, and my body began
experiencing intense energies and contractions that came in increasing
intervals. The closest thing I can compare it to is orgasmic contractions,
which moved up and down through my body until they reached the top
of my head. This started out as a surprising and amusing anomaly but
soon progressed to be uncomfortable and quite painful. I grew more
concerned when it ceased to stop, making it almost impossible for me to
function normally. Later, when I was driving to my home in Colorado
from Santa Fe, I had to stop at a convenience store and buy ice to try to
numb the sensations so that I could drive without having to pull over. I
had no idea I was about to have one of the strangest experiences of my life.

A Very Unusual Encounter on the Side of the Road

I was driving just north of an old hot spring called "Ojo Caliente" when I happened to see an old woman on the side of the road. I was driving quite slowly because of my situation, so I could tell she was looking directly at me. I had driven this road a thousand times before and never seen this woman. She looked as if she were in her eighties and was very small, with weathered skin, gray hair, and somewhat ragged clothes. To the average eye, she looked to be homeless and in the middle of nowhere. Having a special place in my heart for grandmothers and elderly women, and thinking she needed a ride, I pulled over where she was standing and opened the door. She stood there for a moment smiling at me and looking me over, then she climbed into the car and said to me, "You are running a little late, but I'm certainly glad to see you nonetheless." At this point, I figured she was a bit eccentric or maybe even crazy. She then leaned over and took a hold of the medicine bag that I wore around my neck and said in a cheerful voice, "It looks like I've got the right person. You're the one they call 'Child'—Little Grandmother, right?" At this, I sat straight up and began to pay close attention—this was obviously no ordinary old lady. I reached around to the backseat and pulled out some food and offered it to her, thinking she might be hungry. She said, "Oh, sweetie, I don't get hungry . . . put it away."

I pulled onto the highway and asked her where she wanted to go. I told her I was heading to Colorado. She said that she would let me know when she needed to leave. My mind was racing—what was happening? My contraction problem had halted for the last ten minutes or so. I was worried they were going to strike again any minute. I squeezed the ice between my legs a little harder, saying a prayer beneath my breath when she began speaking. Oddly enough, looking back, the whole time she was in the car with me, the strange contractions did not continue.

Though she looked very old, she moved like a fifteen-year-old; she had a great deal of energy and moved with no struggle at all, despite her apparent age. Her voice flowed clearly and strongly. Although her body looked tired and weathered, her eyes sparkled. I'm not saying they had a little sparkle, I'm saying they seemed almost lit up! If you're wondering by now whether she was an apparition or spirit, let me assure you she was very solid and corporeal, just like you and me.

She suddenly spoke: "Why did you pick me up, child?" I answered honestly. I told her how I had never loved anyone as much as I loved my great grandmother, and she, this woman, must be someone's grandma— I couldn't possibly leave her on the side of the road. "Besides," I said, "my heart says you are safe and I was supposed to stop." She smiled and winked at me and said, "I'm glad you are using the senses you were given, that you didn't judge me for the way I look." She told me that I had passed the first test.

While she said this, I kept turning my head from the road to look at her. Her clothes were filthy, her hands had dirt on them, her shoes were hardly staying on because they were so old, and yet the woman smelled like rain. It's the only way I know to describe her scent: she smelled like the forest after a rain in the spring, truly wonderful. She started telling me about the San Luis Valley in which I grew up, how the three prominent mountains (Ute, San Antonio, and Blanca) were very sacred and formed a triangle of energy. Not only does the "serpent of light" (a powerful energy field that creates Mother Earth's chakra system) touch the top of each of these mountains but there are crystal pyramids within each as well as a place where star beings come and go. She said it was no mistake that I was born into this valley surrounded by these three mountains; this land had been teaching me since I was a child and, in a way, feeding my energy with its superenergy so that I could see properly and learn how to listen when I was spoken to from the other side. This, she said, is why she came to speak to me.

She told me that she was called "Lightning Woman" and that she came from "the Black Sea" (I wasn't sure where that was at the time). I asked her how long she'd been here. She said that years to her are not like years to me, that she is ageless. She told me that the Earth was now going through her Great Shift and that the People of the North who had been kept safe from famine, war, and cataclysm must remember their hearts, remember their own Great I AMs. They would be an instrumental part of raising the vibration of love on Mother Earth. She told me it was time I went to these people and awakened their hearts. She also said that Scandinavia would become the breadbasket of the world, a beacon of light if they would awaken, and that they "were ready to be awakened." She spoke of the new energies that would be flowing down to planet Earth. These energies were coming to help human beings digest a higher frequency of light in small amounts, a little at a time, so that we would be prepared for the Great Shift in consciousness when it came. She explained that the human body could not accept the full amount of energy that would come all at once without this. The human beings on the planet right now are those chosen to be here; they are the strongest of the strong of souls who could actually change the world.

She then asked me to pull the car over. There was no road or intersection—it was all open wilderness for miles and miles in all directions. I pulled over and was shocked when she reached over and placed her hand on the ignition switch and the car shut off. There we sat—I had no idea what was coming next. What she said I wouldn't have expected in a million years!

An Intriguing Offer

She told me that at this time on the planet, there are a few beings who are being offered the opportunity to leave, and that if we so choose, we can go to the higher dimension and help our planet by interacting with and assisting those of a higher vibration to understand humanity and how to help humanity during the coming pole shifts. I was one of those being offered this, and this is why she had come.

She told me how there is a large ship that is three miles in circumference within Ute Mountain that has been there for centuries. I would be given passage on the ship to another place (the place she was from?), where I would go to a higher frequency and work with star beings to assist humanity from a higher dimension. In fact, she explained how, wherever there are military bases, within a few miles there are also found bases of star beings. One of these is within the Great Sand Dunes, right over the mountain from the NORAD military complex in the San Luis Valley of Colorado. There is also a great circular valley outside Los Alamos in New Mexico, where a base of star beings exists. In these places, star beings are not necessarily working with the government but are playing an active role in monitoring what is going on, preventing catastrophe and holding a certain vibration to limit the negative potential of what is being done in these places.

She came to tell me all this and to ask me what my decision would be. Did I want to leave planet Earth and this human life and move to a higher dimension of being? I sat there dumbfounded, not knowing what to say. So much was going through my head, and I struggled to make sense of what she was saying for a while. I sat there in deep thought, thinking about my life here on this planet, about my family and the bigger picture: the planet and what was going to happen in the next few years. Could I help if I chose to stay here? What could one person do to be of service? Could I really do anything to make a difference? If I were to leave and assist from a higher place, could I be of greater service? It was such an ironic dilemma to be faced with this choice now.

You see, for years after my beloved great grandmother had died when I was sixteen, I had prayed to leave this world, to go somewhere else. In my early twenties, when I had found out that the man who had sexually abused me was also abusing my disabled brother, I again wanted to leave this Earth life. I could not make sense of what purpose there could be for these things. There were many times in the past at which I had prayed to leave this Earth, and now I was being given the chance.

My head was swimming. It was too much. I began to cry out of fear, anxiety, and confusion, and that is when she hugged me. I had never been hugged like that before. It felt as though I was hugging pure joy, pure love or light, like hugging a smile. She sat back in her seat and began to tell me that she knew what my life had been up until that point. She understood that deep feeling I have had since childhood that this life is not enough, that I struggled with the meaning of things, wanting to know that there is a purpose to it all. I have always felt a deep, indescribable need to live for a purpose, to know that there is a higher meaning, and yet I had no idea how I could do that, and I had always felt lost.

She explained that those things I had been given to experience in my life so far were lessons, a crash course getting me ready for this. She cataloged my learnings thus far: I knew what it was like to be very poor, to be homeless, to live with cruel people, to be physically and sexually abused, to have serious health problems, to be a part of a family with disabled siblings and to learn from them what it means to be pure love beings, to experience the power and abuses of man-made religion and religious brainwashing. She explained how all these things were tests that had led me to have compassion for the abused, the hungry, the homeless, the disabled, the weak and spiritually depressed, and those who are deeply stuck in the old patterns of religion.

My life was a series of lessons, and I had been given these lessons to make me stronger, more compassionate, more understanding. I had made it this far and had passed all these tests. When she was finished speaking, I just sat there with my hands over my face, sobbing, thinking to myself, do I have time to think about this? Does she need an answer immediately? I realized with sudden force that I couldn't possibly leave my children. I'm a *mom*—I couldn't possibly go! I took my hands from my face and looked at her, knowing the answer clearly in my heart.

She told me that she already knew my answer but that she was sent to give me the offer nonetheless—it was in her contract. Then she told me that if I ever needed to talk to her, or if I changed my mind and made the decision to leave, there was a place I could go to find her, very near to where we were pulled over on the side of the road. She told me the exact place to go (with specific markers), what time to arrive, and even who I would meet there and what to ask when I found the place. She explained that I would find a very old man who looks as if he is living on the land with no home and that I should address him as the "Goat Herder." He would tell me where to find her.

She hugged me again and told me she loved me. Then she touched my medicine pouch and my owl talon that I always wear around my neck and smiled. With that, she got out of the car with a childlike sweetness and waved good-bye. I started down the road again, watching her in the rearview mirror, completely expecting her to disappear or be beamed up somehow, but she just stood there until I couldn't see her anymore.

The moment I couldn't see her anymore, the contractions hit me immediately! The feeling of butterflies in my head, my throat and mouth, my stomach, and then between my legs was so intense that it was almost unbearable. One might think having an orgasm every fifteen minutes would be fun, but let me assure you, it is not. Like clockwork, this would overtake my body, and there was nothing I could do about it. Even after the contraction would leave, the feeling of the building energy was already there for the next one. I somehow managed to make it home to Colorado, though I have no idea how I did, especially after my bizarre encounter with this otherworldly being.

Once I got home, these orgasmic contractions did not go away. After three days and nights of them, I was in tears, unable to do anything but lie in my bed. I finally called a healer friend whom I trust deeply as well as a Hopi elder to talk to them about this and ask what I might do to make it stop. I began praying and meditating, trying to focus as best I could while it continued to happen again and again. At this point, they were coming almost every three minutes. And then I had simply had it. I decided to call the doctor and make an appointment, thinking that the doctor must have a shot or some other way to make the contractions stop. It was then, while I was picking up the telephone and dialing the number in tears and frustration, that a knock came at the door. It was a beloved friend who was a shaman and a spiritual elder and who had come to help me.

She told me she was guided to relieve me of the energy flowing through my body. She had received guidance for me that this energy was there for an enormous purpose. It was not only to heal my body of old wounds but to trigger a heightened awareness in my senses. Ultimately, it was to connect me to the kundalini energy of sacred Mother Earth, to rewire me in a sense. I didn't know what the word kundalini meant at the time and asked what she was talking about. The moment she told me, I broke down in tears and asked, "You know what's happening to me?" She nodded with a smile and took me to a back room where I could lie down. She knelt over me and began to chant and to pray. I closed my eyes and melted into a deep meditation.

A Visit from the Kahunas

It was at that time that something amazing happened in the room, just as it had many times before, when I was about to be taught by my spirit guides. Light started to fill the room, small particles of light that eventually formed into several beings. There were three Polynesian-looking men, naked except for cream-colored clothes around their hips. The eldest looked about sixty and was bald, but with long, black hair on the back of his head, tied back. He wore an armband on each arm. The two others were younger and looked about forty, had long hair, and wore armbands and legbands made of plant material. None of the men wore paint or tattoos, though they all wore a white emblem around their necks that looked something like a cross between a fishhook and a spiral.

They told me that they were the kahunas. They were there to ground the energy that I had not figured out how to ground myself. The oldest kahuna began to put what looked like huge banana leaves over my stomach and pelvis, while the others chanted beautifully in some unfamiliar language. The elder kahuna then put some sort of salve, which he scooped out of a porous bowl, on my pelvis and belly, praying as he did so. My friend and elder sister shaman (who could see exactly what was happening) was kneeling nearby and praying as well. I felt the energy in my body shift from the intensity of orgasm into a warm, relaxed feeling. The energy was now flowing through me, both in and out, instead of just in and getting stuck in the sexual chakra. I was told by the kahunas that because of my wounds in this area, I had needed these intense energies to last this long, to heal and rewire me.

The oldest kahuna then explained to me that soon I would be traveling to his land, that I would be called on to open an ancient site of sacred energy that had been closed for many years. He said that I should trust in my guidance and let Mother guide me where I needed to go. He said he would guide me to the place when I arrived on his soil. Little did I know that just a few months later, I would be asked to fly to Maui with a sacred ancient crystal in hand.

A Hope for Our Spiritual Evolution

Experiences such as these have shown me, without a doubt, that this life is far more mysterious than we could ever understand and that we are not alone in the universe; in fact, we are just one of millions of other forms of life. Though we are in our spiritual infancy as a species compared to most other beings in the cosmos, we are much loved by those who helped in creating us. Our evolution is being watched by many races of beings from all over the cosmos and assisted by several species in particular. Star beings were here on Earth in the very beginning, giving us advanced knowledge and technologies and spiritual tools to help us grow and evolve, and they have been coming and going ever since. Yet there have never before been so many beings from elsewhere here on Earth, watching us and helping us both directly and behind the scenes.

Everything I have seen and learned has shown me that the star beings are mostly benevolent and are like parents or big brothers and sisters to us—they care for us deeply and are prepared to help us in any way they can, but we must raise our vibration collectively first. I have been told that these beings from other stars will not come to save us from the changes and transformations that are happening, but they will assist us energetically and in myriad ways from behind the scenes to ensure that we are not destroyed, that we make the evolutionary leap we are destined to make.

As we evolve and raise our frequency, we will be able to see them and communicate with them. Right now, our mass consciousness is still too low for the majority of people to be able to perceive their presence. However, I do believe a time will come when the existence of these beings will no longer be deniable. Knowledge of their presence on Earth and their connection to human beings has been carefully safeguarded by our more advanced ancient ancestors, but it will be brought to the public soon. This will change everything. There will be a full disclosure of who they are and their relationship to us and a bringing forth of the sacred wisdom and knowledge that is ours but that has been lost to us for thousands of years. And this, more than anything, will forever change life on planet Earth.

The Uncovering of Ancient Truths and Wisdom

For the last several years, I have regularly received information about certain places on Earth where there lies hidden knowledge, soon to be revealed to humanity and utilized for our spiritual evolution. I have received spontaneous downloads of information through my picture screen, or sometimes I am directly given information from one of my spirit guides or one or more light beings. When my picture screen opens in front of me, I am shown, sometimes in great detail, places on Earth, names, symbols, and information of an esoteric nature. When this happens, I try to grab my notebook and write down exactly what I see or draw the images and symbols I am being shown. If I do not understand something I am being shown, I am often shown it again. The beings who are teaching me know that I am a simple person, and so I think they attempt to frame this information in ways I can understand.

I cannot say that I always fully understand all of what I have been given or know for what purpose I have been given it, but I share it with you now because it is my responsibility to do so. Some of this information has the power to vastly change our perspective on our own human history, our place in the cosmos, and our spiritual capacity. Much of it relates to our star brethren and advanced spiritual technologies that human beings once knew and have long forgotten. Because I am not a scientist, I offer what I have received as further corroboration of what other seers have been shown to those dedicated explorers who have been studying these places and phenomena, to point them in a fruitful direction for further inquiry. I have meditated on what I am able to share here and offer this information to you in the hope that it will help humanity to remember who we are and rediscover our vast spiritual capacity, that it will enable us to shift into a higher consciousness, along with Mother Earth, when the time comes.

With this information, I was given a specific message from Mother Spirit: "It is time to unbury the ancient truths of men, to prove to all human beings that light beings gave us breath and they have never left us. Look to the hidden knowledge that is being revealed—your eyes are ready to see!" For thousands of years, humanity has been in a state not of evolution but of devolution. We were once far more advanced and knew many things that we have long since forgotten. Those of us here on the planet today are those who are ready to remember the ancient truths, to remember where we really come from and who we have been. The fruit is ripe and ready to fall from the tree. We need but to open our hearts and see.

Uncovering the Pyramids

I have so far received several downloads of information having to do with the pyramids that have been discovered on Earth and how these pyramids clearly show human interaction with star beings. I was specifically shown images of three pyramids in Giza, Egypt, three Mayan pyramids in Mexico, and three pyramids that are buried underwater in an area where the ancient civilization of Atlantis used to be (fifty-five miles off the coast of Florida). These pyramid complexes are star maps, and specific pyramid groupings are perfectly aligned to the stars of Orion's Belt. They were built around 10,500 B.C. by ancient advanced human beings who coexisted with the star beings, using the star beings' technologies of light. There is a hieroglyphic language carved in stone that will be found at each of these places that predates Sanskrit.

Specifically, I was shown that the pyramids were built using sound-energy vibration and antigravity technology. Whereas sound-energy vibration waves move in a figure-8 pattern through creation, the reversal of this pattern creates antigravity. This is also how the ships of star beings operate, through the use of antigravity technology.

In addition, the pyramids are not, as scientists and archaeologists think, simply glorified tombs, symbols of power, or astronomical observatories; rather, they exist to hold a high vibrational frequency on planet Earth that is helping us to evolve. They provide a sound-frequency connection to certain star systems in the cosmos whose inhabitants were involved in the building of the pyramids. We will find that beings from the Pleiades and Sirius have been particularly involved in creating the pyramids. The pyramids emit a frequency that these beings, who were once on Earth and who now continue to visit Earth, need to be here at all. The knowledge of who built the many pyramids that exist all over the planet, and which are still being discovered (and which soon will be acknowledged to exist on the Moon and Mars, as well), is buried in a vast library that will be found under the right paw of the Sphinx in Egypt. Whether this library exists on the three-dimensional level or must be accessed via a higher dimension is not clear.

In this lesson, I was shown a list of places where pyramids from ancient Earth civilizations still stand, where the same ancient inscription will be found. Some of these places have been discovered but are either considered hoaxes by the scientific community or are else vastly misunderstood and underestimated in their antiquity and significance. These pyramids are in Japan (underwater), Utah, Sudan (which contains three pyramids much like those in Giza), Illinois, Greece, Italy (specifically Sicily and Montevecchia were mentioned), Spain, Mexico, Bosnia-Herzegovina, Russia, Egypt (Cairo), the Uyghur region of China, and China proper (where there are over three hundred pyramids and where there is extensive evidence of star beings and UFOs). I was shown that all these pyramids were built with angles corresponding to the placement of Orion's Belt and the Pleiades. Not only are there teachings, writings, and explanations of those who helped build these great pyramids but there are also great and detailed paintings of their ships on the walls of many of these temples that have been barred to the public.

Other Places Where Ancient Truths Will Be Revealed

The ancient, massive temple complex called "Pumapunku" that is part of Tiwanaku in Bolivia is one of the most mysterious places that will soon be revealed to be of cosmic origin. The amazing structures here are characterized by their massive, H-shaped stones, which interlock perfectly. Not only did many of the blocks used weigh more than two hundred tons but there is a precision in the angles and cuts and a uniformity in the blocks and drilled holes that archaeologists and scientists have been unable to explain. The structures were created with a technological and mechanical sophistication that we do not possess even today. I was shown that the drilled holes were created with lasers and diamonds and that the buildings in this complex were built to align, in minutest degree, to the planets in our solar system. They are in actuality more than seventeen thousand years old, and the stone that was used to create the structures is not from Bolivia at all.

In addition, in Dendera in Egypt, evidence of the ancient use of electricity in the form of lightbulbs has been found, and in Greece, ancient computers have already been discovered, with high-tech gears much like the most sophisticated Swiss watches today. What they don't know is that both operated using the advanced knowledge of crystals. We will soon find that there are temples in the ancient Mayan city of Tikal in Guatemala that exactly mirror the alignments of Orion's Belt and Sirius. There is a twin of one of these temples that will be found on the Moon.

The Temple Mount at the Dome of the Rock in Jerusalem, where Solomon's Temple was located, contains unimaginable wisdom. Beneath the Dome of the Rock, light beings have deposited knowledge, and light beings protect that knowledge still today, until humans are ready to accept consciously the knowledge of their origins. This knowledge was put there two thousand years before the Bible was written.

Something else was shown to me that is quite astounding. In Ethiopia, in the middle of nowhere, stands a small, white, stucco church with metal bars around it that is guarded by a blind man who has lived his whole life within its walls. The reason for this is that he guards a most sacred and secret treasure. The man who keeps this sacred treasure was spiritually chosen for this task. He lives his life within this church and is brought food and other necessities by the residents of the village, who all know what is contained there and who are sworn to secrecy. They would never speak to outsiders about it. No one may enter the church, except this chosen guardian. Within a couple days of entering the church, the chosen guardian goes blind—his irises cloud over. When he dies, another is chosen to serve the role of guardian.

What is kept there? Within this church lay what humans understand to be the Ark of the Covenant. I was told that the Ark contains "the laws and knowledge of all life on planet Earth." It was not written by human beings and was created before written language existed. It was originally given to the ancient Assyrians, who coexisted completely with star beings and even traveled with the star beings in their ships. The ancient Assyrians knew where they came from and how they were created. I was told that this knowledge will be revealed to the world in the time of the Great Shift of Mother Earth. With the poles already shifting, we find ourselves living in the most exciting times ever to be witnessed on planet Earth.

In fact, Africa was home to many star beings at the beginning of humanity. Gondwana, located under the sea east of current-day Africa, existed at the time of Atlantis and was one of the primary birthplaces of humanity, along with Israel and other locations in Africa. It was in these places that humans were first created by star beings, beings of a much higher and very loving consciousness.

Fifty-five miles off the coast of Florida are remains of the advanced civilization we now know to be Atlantis. We will soon discover a pyramid there, under the water, that contains artifacts of this civilization. I was told to look for the rings of coral to find the city—old stone buildings, red, black, and white. There is actually an underwater base of light beings there and several large ships that are at least two or three miles long. A massive magnetic field covers this area, containing the sacred energy of life. This is most likely the mysterious area referred to as the Bermuda Triangle, where aircraft and boats have been known to disappear and strange anomalies have been recorded.

I was shown that the ancient stone circle of Stonehenge in England is also a very sacred area and a place used by star beings. There is a force field surrounding Stonehenge that was placed there by light beings. Ancient truths are buried under the ground in the form of hidden tablets. At another time, I was shown that there is a massive ship within the Earth under Stonehenge, and this area of England is an important base for star beings, which is why so many crop circles are found in the area.

All these discoveries, when fully acknowledged and understood, will help to drastically change our perspective about who we once were and what we know as human beings. When I was learning of these things, Mother Spirit appeared and spoke of how "when you add the past to the present, you will know your future." When we remember the ancient ones and what we as humanity once knew, we will be led to a higher consciousness. It is part of the process of how we will speed up and evolve more quickly than any beings in the universe have ever evolved before. We are on the very edge of remembering.

Dolphins, Whales, and the Advanced Creatures

Higher beings live among us in animals—whales, dolphins, elephants—as well as in our ancient trees. Trees such as the redwoods in California are our ancient ancestors and elders who were once living beings on the planet but who have ascended into a higher consciousness. They then made the choice to return to Earth to hold a certain frequency for us. Whereas the ancient trees are our Earth ancestors, the dolphins are actually more advanced beings from elsewhere in the cosmos. The Mayans, Dogon people, and Aborigines all have knowledge of these beings from the stars that we call "dolphins." The Dogon tribe of Mali in West Africa recognizes them as Nommos in their mythology, fishlike human creatures who descended from the sky. These beings came from a large disk of light and were born into the sea.

I have been taught that the Nommos come from a very small star that rotates around Sirius A every forty-nine years. The very first fish symbol used by the ancient peoples of Earth was a symbol of the Nommos, the beings from the stars. Later this symbol was adapted and used by Christianity, but its first form was a representation of these beings from the stars who were born into our oceans. Their lives are dedicated to helping humanity, to holding a high vibration to help us evolve.

Right now, there is a delicate balance; if humanity can raise its consciousness, the star beings will stay here on Earth, but if we continue to damage Mother Earth and each other, they will leave, as some are already leaving. They cannot live in a lower frequency. Human beings have finally begun to understand that dolphins and whales have special gifts to give human beings and that they are highly intelligent and advanced creatures. Being in their energy fields can heal human beings such as we have seen with autistic children and people with other serious disabilities. Their loving nature and intelligence have been acknowledged by even the most traditional scientists.

Elephants have gotten less attention for their intelligence and spiritual capacities. Like dolphins, they, too, use a sonar to communicate. Their spiritual frequency is just as high as that of dolphins and whales, and they are here to help us. It is important to preserve their habitats and honor these creatures—as we destroy them, we destroy ourselves. It is no exaggeration to say that these special beings are here to keep a high enough frequency on planet Earth so that we do not destroy ourselves or Mother Earth.

Our military equipment and underwater technologies that use sonar are extremely damaging to these special creatures who use sonar to communicate. If we knew how sacred and important these creatures were to our survival on Earth, we would not so casually hunt them and destroy their habitats with our technologies, treating the oceans and jungles as dumping grounds and as limitless resources for our shortsighted use.

Practice: Using Earthly and Heavenly Energies for Awakening

I am often taught about sacred geometry and how energy moves in patterns through creation. Though some of this is far too complex for me to try to explain (and sometimes to understand!), I was taught a particular energy meditation through my picture screen that uses the energies of Earth and heaven to activate one's Great I AM, also referred to as one's lightbody—which is based on the six-pointed star. Drunvalo Melchizedek is a very special spiritual teacher in our time who has devoted years to helping human beings activate their lightbodies, which were called the Mer-Ka-Ba by the ancients. While I recommend learning more about activation of the Mer-Ka-Ba from someone like Drunvalo, who has been given special knowledge of the science of the Mer-Ka-Ba and who truly knows what he is doing, I would like to offer this practice as it was given to me. Because I am simple and not scientific, perhaps this practice was pared down and made simple so I would understand it and be able to use it and share it. It may be useful for those of you who also need a very simple kind of visualization.

In this meditation, the six-pointed star, which represents the union of heaven and Earth, masculine and feminine, is created by two pyramids, one pointing up toward heaven, representing the male or Father energy, the other pointing down to Earth, representing the feminine. Imagine these two pyramids of light overlapping your body, intersecting each other in the region of your belly, your sexual chakra. The upward pointing pyramid is made of gold light. The light descends from the crown chakra at the top of your head and spins counterclockwise. The downward pointing pyramid is made of green light. This light ascends from Mother Earth through the bottom of the feet and spins clockwise. As you breathe, imagine these pyramid forms of light spinning in opposite directions, uniting the Earth and sky, Mother and Father, in your center. Feel the gratitude and love for both Mother Earth and Great Spirit as these energies circulate around and within you and merge around your midsection. As you start to connect to your higher self, you will begin to feel warmth and a kind of ecstasy flowing through you. When you start to feel this, if you start thinking or become self-conscious of what is happening, you may lose it. Try to stay in the feeling until you feel a sense of expansion and of becoming wholly light. It may be helpful to start with one of the pyramids, to start it spinning before you overlay the other pyramid. If visualizing a three-dimensional pyramid spinning in space is difficult for you, try using a funnel shape, more like a tornado. When I do this practice, I work on gradually expanding the spinning light pyramids so that they reach out into space farther and farther.

This practice, though challenging at first, will raise your spiritual frequency more than any other practice I have ever been given. It is a key to connecting with the universal consciousness and to your Great I AM.

Global Changes Happening and to Come

Do you remember the news reports and sightings of blue spirals in the sky in Utah, Colorado, Norway, and Russia in 2009? These were covered by major news media, but as usual, they were written off as explainable phenomena by some lone scientific or government expert. The most significant of these spirals, witnessed by thousands in Norway and filmed or photographed by hundreds, was explained away as the result of a Russian missile test. These spirals had been appearing in the skies since 2006, but in 2009, we saw a flurry of them appear all over the planet. Back in 2009, before the spirals began appearing, I was called to a meeting of wisdom keepers with one of our wise indigenous spiritual elders. We were told that we would be entering a period of new energies coming to the planet that had not been seen since ancient times. These energies would be seen in the skies in the form of spirals. Science would try to come up with an explanation and would try to tell people what to believe. Yet millions would see them, and there would be no hiding them. I was later shown through my picture screen that these spirals have to do with the return of the ancient ones, the star beings. They act as a kind of high-frequency portal to our world. They are proof that new, higher energies are coming to planet Earth to help us raise our frequency. They are certainly not man-made, regardless of what governments and the media reported. In reality, science has no idea what causes these brilliant and amazing spirals of light. They are not man-made, and they are not just some quirky anomaly.

In 2009, spirals were seen in the skies of Brazil, Norway, China, Russia, Canada, Iran, Utah, Nebraska, Uzbekistan, Mexico, and England. But why a spiral? How is it that the same light blue spiraling light was seen all over the world? Why is the spiral one of the most, if not the most, prehistoric and ancient symbols on Earth, found in every indigenous culture across the globe? There were no telephones, no e-mail, no printing presses in ancient times. Yet almost every ancient culture considers the spiral a sacred symbol.

For the Celts and the Norse from the north, the spiral was a symbol of eternity and of the Goddess; for the Greeks and Romans, it signified oneness and unity; for African cultures, it signified the womb, the Great Mother and Goddess; for cultures in the Orient, it signified the beginning of all life, where the gods come from; and in India, it signified the One and contained the Fibonacci sequence found in all nature. Native American cultures, such as the Hopi, regarded the spiral as the circle of life; the Mayans also saw it as such. For the Polynesians, it meant immortality. But why did all these cultures recognize the spiral? The answer is simple: no one taught them about the spiral; rather, they saw them in the skies.

Every ancient culture on this planet actually saw the spiral. The spiral appears when cosmic energies pour down on the Earth, at a pivotal time of spiritual evolution. It is the sign of the light beings—the star beings— and most ancient peoples knew who they were and had encountered them. The ancient ones remembered seeing these spirals before, at the time of the last great shifting of Earth. They saw them in the skies, and now we are seeing them again, reminding us of our place in the cosmos and of the existence of something much greater in the universe than we have previously understood. The appearance of these spirals, after thousands of years, is yet another sign that the great prophesied shifting of Mother Earth and human consciousness in our age has begun.

For our life on planet Earth to really change, to be driven by Love rather than power, greed, and ego, some deep global changes are going to have to happen that will change the way we perceive our lives and our human societies. Right now, much information and even truths about who we are and what we are capable of are being hidden from the public by governments and powerful entities who do not want to lose control or lose profit. You would be amazed to know what is being kept hidden, for some of this knowledge would free human beings to live more equitably and would help us to provide for every human being on this planet. It would also awaken us to the truth of where we come from, who else is out there in the universe with us, and what we are capable of.

However, there is one big problem with these spiritual truths being revealed to the masses of humanity. With just one irrefutable disclosure of this nature, one proof of our cosmic origins, most of the major religions would become unnecessary, would be seen as what they are: man-made. Our conceptions of the universe and of God would be blown wide open. Think of how powerful religion is on this planet, how it rules the lives of so many beings, controlling vast amounts of wealth and exerting profound political influence: do you think the major religions want this knowledge to be brought out?

The three things that control the life of just about every human being on the planet are money, government, and religion. Since 2009, the wisdom keepers have been receiving a similar message about what is coming. We are being shown that before human beings can shift into a higher consciousness, big religion, big government, and big money will have to fail—and they will. Right now these things are actually working together to prevent human beings from stepping into who they truly are, from creating a world ruled by the heart. Right now governments are keeping the children of Mother Earth separate from each other and divided, just as religion is, just as the multinational corporate empires and greed-driven power brokers are. The balance of power in this world has been controlled by a handful of immensely powerful people for a very long time. They know exactly what information must not be brought out to the people, and there are deep and hidden alliances between religion, government, and big business that most people have no clue about.

For example, I was shown in detail on my picture screen an invention that exists, that sits surrounded by a dark sea. It looks like a tall, thin pyramid made of wires and cables, with a large bulb or ball on top. It seems to pull energy or light from the sky. This has been made already and is capable of supplying a great part of the world's energy. It was created, I believe, by Nicola Tesla. Yet it has been kept hidden for years and is being controlled by politics and its ties to big business. Those in power do not want to create a free energy source for all human beings. But soon it will be revealed and made public, as the structures that govern our lives begin to lose power and fall.

Religion has controlled whole populations and has covert financial and business dealings as well as ties to politics that do not benefit the masses of human beings. There have been more killings and wars in the name of religion than almost anything else. All these illusory divisions are created among human beings so that we are mindlessly led to think of some human beings as the enemy or of whole nations of people as unworthy or somehow expendable. For the planet to become a beautiful state in which we all love each other as brothers and sisters, and in which we treat each other with kindness and compassion, these illusory divisions among human beings will have to be eradicated.

Some of our most basic structures of government, religion, and money will start to fail. And when one fails, the others will fail, too, in a domino effect, because they are all deeply connected. There will be a kind of leveling of the playing field on a global level, and economically as well. Some countries that are very powerful now will not be so in the future. The governance of the world will undergo a reorganization. This will happen in large part because of economic forces and realities that are now being downplayed. I have been shown on my picture screen the global currency that will be the currency of the future world. It has already been manufactured. I am not sure when exactly this will come into use, but it will. Other wisdom keepers have also seen this.

All these changes will not necessarily be scary—some may happen more smoothly than you might imagine. People who are attached to the status quo and to their wealth may have a hard time adjusting to changes in the system. But the changes are going to come so that humanity can have a fresh start—so that we can create a better, more equitable and just world. Some of these changes will not happen by choice but because of crises that will occur. Yet in the future, we will see them as the godsend they will be. The old structures have to fall before new structures can be set in place. The fall of some of our basic economic and political structures, and even of our sense of basic security, will help us open our consciousness and advance quite rapidly. Our eyes will be opened—and what matters most to us now will not matter in the future. Our priorities will change, as our lives and societies will change.

These are real possibilities that I and other wisdom keepers have seen for the future; however, the key is that we shift our global human consciousness from mind and ego back to heart, to Love. Whether we need to be shaken for this to happen or whether we can shift more gently is up to us. I feel that we have a choice collectively, and how this shift in human consciousness comes about is being affected each day by the choices we make, by the energy we create. This is why it is important to return to loving Mother Earth, to give time each day to developing a loving consciousness, and to follow the dictates of your heart and higher self in how you choose to live now. We are creating, each day, how the future will unfold. Whatever happens, we must remember that it is for the purpose of creating a more beautiful world, allowing human beings to join together and unify as one heart, as the children of Mother Earth, as the family we were meant to be.

The Great Shifting of Mother Earth

One of the reasons I have been asked to gather the Tribe of Many Colors and to share the messages and information I have been given is to help prepare humanity for the unbelievable shift that is prophesied to happen within a window of the next few years on planet Earth. You have probably all heard about December 21, 2012, being the end-date of the five-thousand-year-old Mayan calendar. You may also know that this remarkable date also corresponds to a very rare cosmic event that happens only every twenty-six thousand years. The precession of the equinox happens when our sun and Earth come into rare alignment with the center of the galaxy. Can you believe you are alive to witness a cosmic event that has not occurred for twenty-six thousand years?

Nearly all indigenous people's prophecies, including the Maya and the Hopi, agree that something massive is due to happen on Earth at this time, something that will change the entire path of human development. All the indigenous spiritual elders, advanced beings, and wisdom keepers on the planet right now are receiving a similar vision from Spirit and from Mother Earth herself—we are in the midst of a Great Shift on planet Earth that will bring with it destruction of the old and herald a new age. I have been told by Spirit that very soon, Mother Earth will shift into her high heavenly self and that human beings are being given an opportunity to go with her into a higher dimension. It is a pivotal moment of collective choice for humanity. Will we continue on our destructive, blind, life-killing path, or will we radically change the consciousness of humanity and start living from the heart, once again in harmony with Mother Earth?

If there is any reason that I have been given the task of gathering the Tribe of Many Colors and sharing this message with you, it is for this sole reason: what we do now, and how we prepare ourselves, is more important than we can imagine. The fate of humanity depends on how we will respond to this cosmic opportunity. We are being asked to re-member who we are and to start living from the heart again, to change the ruling consciousness on planet Earth from ego and mind to Love, from polarity to unity consciousness. If anything will save us and help us move with Mother Earth into a more ascended way of being, it is this. And yet the changes will happen whether or not we are ready for them. So what is it exactly that is likely to happen?

Science has evidence that a magnetic pole shift occurred on Earth thirteen thousand years ago, and another thirteen thousand years before that. At the time before the last pole shift, the Hudson Bay was actually the location of the north pole. This last pole shift corresponds to the time of the Great Flood that has been recorded by all the world's mythologies and religions. This also marks the time when Atlantis, that mythical continent that has been written about by Plato, Herodotus, and many thinkers, psychics, and visionaries, sank into the sea. The Atlanteans lived through that pole shift, when the magnetic north pole shifted its location on the Earth. Many died in the cataclysms that followed, but the most spiritually advanced (the priests) among them knew well in advance that this would occur and began leaving Atlantis for other lands, taking with them their spiritual knowledge and technologies. There are to this day human beings who trace their history back to Atlantis. After the last pole shift, when Atlantis began to sink, the priests got on their boats and sailed to South America. The Mayans are the direct descen-dants of the Atlanteans.

To this day, the Mayans are the only people alive who remember liv-ing through the last pole shift. Though many books have been written about the Mayan calendar and Mayan prophesy, the Mayans themselves only began speaking to the world about a year ago. One of their most esteemed elders and representatives, Don Alejandro Oxlaj, also called "Wandering Wolf," is a thirteenth-generation Quiche Mayan high priest and leader of the national Mayan Council of Elders of Guatemala. He has begun sharing with the world what is likely to happen in the next few years, as the Earth prepares once again for her magnetic poles to reverse and the physical poles of the Earth to shift to new locations.

Though I do not want to try to represent here what the Mayans are saying about 2012, I'd like to share with you what I have directly received about it from Spirit. Much of what I have been shown agrees with what the Mayans are saying and also with some of what Edgar Cayce, the "Sleeping Prophet" who was astoundingly accurate in his predictions, saw. I know that many people are concerned about what such a shift might mean to us here on Earth and for our communities and families.

First, though I have been shown images and received specific information about the pole shift that will occur, I have never been given a specific date. Even the Mayans say that there is a window of opportunity during which the shift could occur, a period in which we are now living, which began about 2007 and extends to 2015. There is evidence that previous pole-shifting processes began hundreds of years earlier, with the weakening of Earth's magnetic field. We do know that Earth's magnetic field has indeed been weakening for about the last five hundred years and dramatically over the last few decades. We also know that the magnetic poles are already shifting. "Due north" is not due north on the compass anymore. Many airports all over the world have had to change the settings for "due north" on their equipment, and migratory birds are getting lost for the first time on their migration routes. The poles are shifting. They will not stop until it is complete.

I have been told that the new location of the north pole will be 17 degrees into Russia and that the geographic shifting of the poles will take about twenty hours to complete. During the actual final physical shift, the crust of the Earth will move, but the core will hold steady. The magma beneath the crust will act somewhat like grease on a ball bearing and will allow the crust to move and shift. This shift will be followed by anywhere from twenty-four to thirty-six hours of total darkness. During this time, we are advised to stay as calm and as inwardly focused as possible. When we are in the middle of this dimensional shift, what you think will become real—fears will become amplified and will become manifest, just as Love and positive emotions such as gratitude and compassion will become manifest in what you see around you. In higher dimensions, the distance between thought and reality is much less, so be very mindful of keeping your spiritual vibration high and not giving in to fear. The more you can be comfortable going within into meditation or a prayerful state of consciousness, the more calm and relaxed you will be, the more open to guidance and intuition. What I have been instructed is to trust that the light will return and to stay centered in Love.

When the light returns, your location on Earth will have shifted, though you will be on the same landmass. You may be in a new hemisphere with a very different climate. Will there be earthquakes, volcanoes, flooding, and a breaking apart of some landmasses? Yes. However, humanity will survive. There will be some destruction and loss of life from natural disasters, but humanity will survive. Later I will share exactly what I have seen, for you to do with what you will, but you must trust your own heart and inner guidance. Each of us has intuitions, visions, and premonitions, and it is up to you to follow your own higher self. I share what I have seen as something that is possible, but I do believe that our consciousness and what we choose collectively in the coming days can change the future, can alter what will happen and how.

During this time, we will be shifting from the third dimension into the fourth, as Mother Earth herself will. This is what the Great Shift is really about. It is not just about the physical world shifting and changing, it is about human consciousness moving into a higher dimension. It is such an exciting time to be alive. We are going to witness the greatest transformation possible, and when it is finished, we will be living in a new world. In the future, there will be a rebirth of Universal Love on planet Earth, and we human beings will accomplish near-miraculous feats. We just need to be able to make it through the eye of the storm that will come before the rainbow. We need to let the old be destroyed so that the new can be born. We may see some people leaving the planet and a higher level of chaos and instability before the shift is complete, but in the face of it, we need to keep our hearts and eyes attuned to the beauty that is coming, to the great promise of new life and of a kind of heaven on Earth.

Know that you are actually a being of light and that your physical form is just the smallest aspect of what you are. Attune yourself to the heart of Mother Earth, and remember that you are the creator of your reality. Whatever happens outside, you have a choice how to respond and on what to focus your consciousness. Know that what will be when the light returns is more beautiful than you can imagine. Keep your heart vibration as high as possible, which will keep you connected to Mother Earth, the sun, and the universe. Feelings of gratitude and love will keep you connected to the living heart of Mother and to your own Great I AM. Do not give in to fear or fantasies of what may happen. Surrender and ride the wave, without having to understand what is happening. Know that you will be fine and well, and expect miracles. Try to have the curiosity of a child and a sense of total openness to life.

Human beings once were much more spiritually advanced than we are today. At the time of Atlantis, we knew how to use sound, color, and energy to heal ourselves. We understood more about our place in the cosmos and the laws of creation that govern all life. We had technologies, both spiritual and scientific, that we cannot even fathom today. We *know* how to do these things. The memory is buried within our DNA. We just need to remember what we once knew, remember who we really are.

It is important to understand that all of us who are on Earth now as human beings have chosen to experience this amazing moment of transformation. We are the strongest of the strong—and our souls are needed here at this time. We are those beings born to a world ruled by mind, separateness, and ego, who are capable of saying, "We want more." We are the ones who will change the world by remembering who we really are as divine beings. We chose to be alive during this time on Earth, to have this initiation, to create a new world. Many of us here today have a role to play that is very important. Remember that you are here for a great purpose! You are much larger than you can possibly realize. It is important to hold in your heart an image of Love and Beauty, to know that you are the creator of your reality. In the future, this will be even more true, and we will step into our true spiritual capacities as human beings. We will leave polarity consciousness and enter unity consciousness. We will leave behind the sense of separation born of ego and know that we are pure consciousness, able to manifest anything.

People, of course, want to know whether we will still have physical bodies after the shift. It seems likely that we will continue to have bodies but that they will not be as dense as they are in our current, three-dimensional Earth life. We will have light bodies and will be able to do things that we can now only imagine such as walking through walls, communicating through telepathy, and traveling anywhere we need to be through our consciousness. This is where we are headed; whether this will be accomplished directly as a result of the pole shift or in the years afterward, when we move into the fifth dimension of Universal Love, has yet to be revealed.

Though no one knows exactly what will happen during this Great Shift and the time preceding, I have been shown that there will be natural cataclysms and an increasing chaos because of Earth events that will occur as well as some radical changes in our governments and economic systems. Whether this will happen before or after the actual pole shift I have not been shown specifically, but it seems likely that these things will happen before the final shifting of the Earth.

In 2008, I was shown on my picture screen a map of the United States (Turtle Island) and some specific areas that would be affected during the time of the Great Shift. I share these with you now, for your information, but truly encourage you to trust your own intuition about where you need to be. You are always a co-creator of your reality, and each one of us has signed on for a different purpose. Even if you live in an area that will be affected by Earth changes, you will not necessarily come to harm. Some of us may have a soul purpose in being in a certain place and have a role to play that we came here to experience. You must trust your heart and follow your own guidance about where you are meant to be, knowing that there is a divine purpose in everything.

I feel it is my responsibility to share here what I have seen, even though I do not want to incite fear and I was not given a particular timeline when shown these things. I was shown that the easternmost areas of the U.S. East Coast, from New York to Florida, would be affected by rising water levels. The areas along the shoreline would be most affected, including the whole of New York City. This is true for the West Coast as well. Areas close to the shoreline would be in danger, with rising sea levels. Lands west of the Rocky Mountains would be affected by coming Earth changes. I saw the Great Lakes actually spilling out as if they were being tipped forward and this water forming a channel down to the Gulf of Mexico, swelling the Mississippi River. Places directly in this path were inundated with water. I was also shown an island in the Pacific that I now know to be Japan facing particular calamity. I saw the entire island covered with water and sinking. I have also been told, at various times, that places near or surrounded by mountains would be protected, and places farther inland (excluding the lands directly beneath the Great Lakes down to the Gulf of Mexico) would be safer in general than the coastlines. Places that are near or below sea level will be most at risk for flooding. Cities will be less safe than rural areas in the face of increasing earthquakes, flooding, and other Earth events.

Because Mother Earth is the heart chakra of the universe, when she begins her Great Shift, it will affect all other planets in our solar system, as well. As our consciousness changes, so will the entire solar system. Some of these phenomena have been occurring since 2008 and have been detected by science. Venus will become much brighter. Mars will become warmer and warmer, just as Earth is, and the ice caps there will melt. A huge red spot on Jupiter will appear, as the plasma becomes more charged. Mercury will experience magnetic tornadoes. New rings will appear around Saturn. Uranus and Neptune will get brighter and experience huge storms, while Pluto, which is moving away from the sun, will also go through global warming and experience greater atmospheric pressure. As Mother Earth's frequency rises, and the human frequency rises along with it, the whole solar system, of which we are a microcosm, will follow suit.

Though it is tempting to feel fear about these Earth changes and the shifting of the poles that is prophesied to come, we must remember that all these things are the labor pangs required to birth a new world. We will be asked to let go of those things we do not truly need and that have kept us imprisoned in a very limited way of being. As we see certain structures fall around us, we will realize that these walls that fall are the very walls that have kept us in prison and separated us from each other, from the truth of who we really are. We will come into a higher Truth as humanity, and we will at last be able to create the kind of world we know is possible.

Those old structures that governed our lives have to fall before we can begin anew. It is an amazing gift to be alive and a child of Mother Earth at this exact moment. The entire universe is watching what is happening on planet Earth. We are about to ascend in consciousness as a species, and Mother Earth is about to be reborn. Do not hold on to what is old and passing away. Let your heart be open to the divinity of each moment you are given, to the Love you have for this planet, this existence, for all the precious beings in your life, for this chance to be here. Stay in Love, and know that you will be protected. All is happening as your Great I AM planned before you came here. You will always exist. Things change form, but it is an expansion, not a lessening of being, that is coming to us. There is nothing to fear. When everything settles and the light returns, you will see with new eyes, and the Beauty you see will melt your heart with gratitude and awe. You will hear the sweet strains of a song more beautiful than you can imagine. It is the song of the soul of Earth and her beautiful children that you already know in your heart, that you will finally remember—that was the whole reason why you came here.

The Way of the Tribe of Many Colors

Imagining a Beautiful World

The key to our spiritual evolution and survival on planet Earth at this time is to *remember who we are*. We are divine co-creators of our reality. We are all the Great I AM. What we dream with our hearts has more power than we realize. The aboriginals have never lost this wisdom and understand that this three-dimensional reality we assume to be so concrete and real is really much like a dream. Just as anything can happen in a dream, and things can be materialized and transformed within an instant, we can transform our reality through the power of our dreaming.

The images and ideas we hold in our minds first exist in the realm of imagination and thought, then become materialized. If you really think about this, what it means is that we first must be able to visualize something existing before it can exist. The more detailed and concentrated one's imagining is, the stronger the image becomes. When this focused, dedicated imagining from the heart is matched with emotion and a high vibratory state of consciousness, when one experiences one's Great I AM, then one can create anything. It is our obligation now to reclaim this divine capacity that we have always had as human beings. We must remember that we are co-creators and that it is up to us to imagine a beautiful new world in as much detail as we possibly can.

Certain images born in just one human heart can inspire global change. Inspiration comes when the heart is moved to new heights and new possibilities are glimpsed. This is the state we need to be in collectively. The Tribe of Many Colors is just such an image, a collective inspiration. For hundreds of years, many indigenous cultures have spoken about the coming of a Rainbow Tribe during this period of dramatic change on Earth. Brothers and sisters of every color, race, nationality, and tongue would come together in unity as children of one Mother, Mother Earth. This would be a heart recognition, not connected to any particular religion or tradition. These people would be the ones capable of changing the world, of *being* the change needed. These people are those who are ready to start living from the heart and who are ready to be in a whole new way. This is the Tribe of Many Colors, and you who are reading this probably already know that you are one of this tribe.

We need to envision a better, more beautiful world, a better humanity—and we can seed that vision from heart to heart through the power of our inspired dreams. It is important to do this as often as you can, when you have raised your energy and are vibrating in Love. Imagine what you want to see. Imagine what could be, in detail. Don't hold yourself back now—if you are inspired to write songs, to write poems or essays giving a glimpse of this new Earth, to make art or give voice to your visions, the time is now. Be as creative as you can, and think outside the box. How can you inspire hearts to remember who they are? How can you seed the vision of something more beautiful in the world? Go into your heart and find the image that will touch other hearts in recognition. Nurture it and water it with your love.

The more of us who choose to live from our hearts and from Love, the more we will open new possibilities for our future on planet Earth. We know that the way we live here on Earth together has to change. We are on the brink of destroying ourselves and the basis of all life on the planet. It is time for us all to believe in our deepest dreams and visions and to feed them through focused attention and love, every day. The future is still a grid of possibilities in which many things exist in potential form. Our future is there for us to choose, to envision. We really can affect the outcome of things, can change destiny through the power of our heartfelt thoughts, feelings, and dreams. It is time to be mindful of that to which we are giving our energy, of the images we are holding in our minds. Do not be afraid that you are being silly to imagine a new world; we are children of this planet, and we are active participants in what shall happen here.

There is a place that is always available to us that can be reached in meditation, where one can merge with the All. In this space, you become merged with creation, with the cosmos, with the mind of God—and from here, whatever you need or wish can be created. Here there is no time, no space, no form; there is only pure unity consciousness. There is no beginning or end. Here there is no separation between things; you can speak to anyone or anything that exists, anywhere in the cosmos. There is no distance between consciousness and manifestation. The moment you are conscious of something, it is given life. From here you may enter a place between the worlds where time collapses and space expands into infinity. The veils between the dimensions dissolve.

I have experienced that this is the space where you can create anything, can ask for anything from your higher self and it will be given. But ironically, when you enter this space, you will see the perfection of everything and know the outcome and purpose of all that is. From this cosmic perspective, which encompasses past and future and sees the many dimensions of existence, all our limited desires and personal goals dissolve. There is no need to change things because everything is unfolding in perfection. Several times I have tried to bring my desires into this space to manifest a particular thing and found that they had become utterly insignificant. I could not even remember what it was my smaller self wanted so much!

So before you enter this consciousness, imagine with the mind of God what kind of world you would like to see. Imagine something worthy of your highest spiritual being, worthy of the human heart. When you enter into this empty black space of the All, what will you bring into being? I often imagine a time when human beings truly feel their oneness of being with the Earth, all her creatures, and each other. We take care of each other and want to share any abundance or goodness we have. All the false boundaries are broken down, and we come into a new kind of human family. We live not for what will make the most profit or give the most prestige but for what will increase the overall beauty, health, and happiness of all beings. This includes our precious Mother Nature. Because we do not feel small and limited anymore, there is no need to serve one's own ego or to protect what is one's own. Because we are no longer motivated by greed, we use all our creativity and intelligence to solve the problems we face. We find solutions; we find a way to live in harmony with nature and to feed everyone on the planet. It is a universal law that the more loving you are, the more intelligent you become. When we become more loving, we will find the answers to our problems.

We will create small communities of interdependence and once again live in close intimacy with Mother Earth, treating her as sacred. We will no longer feel driven to buy things and keep ourselves isolated and protected; rather, we will create things and realize that love is the only true currency of any value. Whatever we do, we will do it out of highest love, and this love will create a real paradise on Earth.

Though this vision may seem far-fetched and idealistic right now, in the future, it will simply be the way things are. I know this in my heart, and know that it will come about through shifting the consciousness of humanity from mind to heart and from moving into a higher dimension with Mother Earth. This is our human destiny, if we are to stay here on planet Earth. There really is no other way. Now is the time to let your imagination soar and to trust what your heart is telling you about what is possible.

Sending Prayers and Gratitude to Mother Earth

I have said many times that Mother Earth is a living spirit, a being who feels us and responds to us, just as we can feel her. Right now she is going through a kind of cleansing and is trying to heal herself from the imbalances and damage that we human beings have caused. She is also preparing to undergo a Great Shift, a transformation that has not happened for many millennia. Through this great shifting, she will be reborn into her heavenly self, I have been told. In preparation for this, she is shifting and stretching, receiving much energy from the heavens to assist her. She will survive her great transformation and become healed and whole again because she is precious to the whole universe. She is the heart chakra of the whole universe. In this sense, she doesn't need our prayers—she will go on with or without us. But our prayers do affect her; they affect the entirety of creation, which is pure energy and consciousness; and most important, they deeply affect us.

When we give our prayers and heartfelt gratitude to Mother Earth, we connect to her—we become united with her heart. We feel her love in return. Through tuning our hearts to Mother Earth and sending her our love, we open the channel to our higher selves and can feel the love we are constantly receiving, that is all around us. We ground ourselves deeply and open ourselves to guidance from the cosmos, the stars, and realms of light. But how does one pray to Mother Earth, to that which is all around us and within us?

I don't think there is one way to pray or that you have to follow any particular tradition—the important thing is to use your heart to guide you and to connect to her. When I pray, the most important thing for me is that I feel what I am saying and that I am totally sincere in that moment. Some people are more comfortable with meditation than prayer because of early religious training that did not touch the heart with truth. Although there is no correct way to pray, I often start by reciting the many things for which I am thankful. Gratitude is the key that unlocks the heart. The more specific you can be, the better. It always helps me to tune in to the details of my day and all the small beauties I have seen and received. It is helpful to speak these things out loud. Some people may find that they can just as easily offer an inward prayer, just by taking a moment to appreciate and say a thank-you inwardly for some small gift of beauty: a beautiful wildflower, a heartfelt interaction with a stranger, a delicious meal. Whether you pray inwardly or outwardly, the most important thing is to feel a welling up of love in your heart and a sense of gratitude for this life. When you feel this strongly, and your emotion has been unlocked, then you can direct your prayers toward a specific purpose or area of creation that needs healing.

When you pray to Mother Earth as a whole to be healthy, it is important to imagine her in her beautiful, healthy, clean state. If you are praying to help heal a specific problem, you can imagine the illness as a particular color and then use another color to heal the illness. For example, if you are sending love and prayers for healing to the waters and creatures of the Gulf of Mexico, rather than focusing on the oil spill and the damage done, picture the waters clean, alive, and healthy. Send your love and compassion to the creatures and the waters, but do not give energy to the problem; instead, imagine the waters as they might be, in their pure state, or imagine the transformation of toxins into something beneficial. For the last year or so, a global community of people has been meditating and praying for Mother Earth at the same time every day, at noon Mountain Standard Time. When many hearts gather at the same time to direct their prayers and energy toward something positive and beautiful, it is extremely powerful. The effects of our prayers multiply, and we really do affect the consciousness of the planet. We can use our divine co-creative powers to *envision* healing and love and bring it into being. We can affect what happens on Earth by holding a high vibration, allowing for the highest possible outcome to manifest. Most important, taking time to remember and pray for Mother Earth each day will make you aware of your connection to all life and bring you naturally into gratitude for your body, for this precious environment in which we live, for the gift of life and creation.

When we feel gratitude in our hearts, our hearts are open and flowing. You cannot truly feel gratitude without your heart opening. It is not a thought but a feeling. When you feel this state, your entire energy changes. You become tuned to more subtle energies around you and within you. Your sense of separate self or ego lessens, and you notice the little things that before you took for granted. This is the state in which you are open to spontaneous blessings and intuition. When you are not so caught up in ideas of who you are, you can open to a much larger reality. In this state, you can see, feel, hear, and sense much more. You can open to guidance from your higher self. You can become a conscious creator of reality.

Giving Back Crystals to Mother Earth

At the end of 2010, I received a very special message from Mother Earth to share with all her children. Never before have I received a direct request from her. She never asks anything from her children, so please hear this message with your openhearted attention. For too long, we have taken crystals and precious stones out of the body of the Earth. Though crystals are meant to be used by human beings for healing and awakening, many crystals that are in human possession are not being consciously used. They are sitting on shelves and under glass cases collecting dust. Mother Earth is asking that we give these crystals back to her—but in a very special way. She is asking that we put our loving prayers and intentions into these crystals, that we pray for her healing and rebirth. This can be done simply by holding a crystal in your hand and getting into a meditative or prayerful state of consciousness. When you are grounded and feel connected to your higher self, imagine what you wish for Mother Earth, for the whole of creation. Say your prayer inwardly or outwardly, but focus your intention and send this thought or feeling into the crystal. You should feel it with your heart, with your emotion. Let your love radiate into the crystal. Then give the crystal back to wild water—any water that is moving such as a river, stream, bay, sea, or ocean.

If you are wondering why we are being asked to place these crystals, embedded with our prayers, into wild water, the answer is quite beautiful and simple. Earth is a water planet and, like the human body itself, is made primarily of water. Water is the fastest conductor of energy and frequency. The intentions placed within the crystals go directly into Mother's blood and spread over the planet. And unlike any other element, water does something extraordinary: it evaporates. When the water carrying our prayers evaporates, the prayers are taken up into the air and are carried by the winds. Then those water particles form clouds, and when it rains, the prayers rain down on the Earth, touching every living thing—every tree, stone, plant, being. What a brilliant way to infuse the entirety of creation with our Love and our healing prayers!

So I ask you, and have been asking everyone since the beginning of 2011, to please give back those crystals you are not using, embedded with your prayers, carrying your deepest, heartfelt love. Mother Earth needs them now. Give her your gratitude—program your crystals with the intensity of your love for her, for this beautiful planet we have been given, for these bodies and this miraculous Earth life. It is something so simple and direct that we can do for her—to help her go through her Great Shift. I have been sharing this message all over the planet, and so far, I have seen thousands of people heed the call in beautiful ways. Create your own sacred ceremony—do it alone or with a group of other unified hearts. The key is to pour your feelings, intentions, and love into the crystals and to let these crystals vibrate through the living blood of

Mother. Brother or sister, through this one act alone, you can have a profound effect on our world and can affect the future. I hope you will join me in this sacred task.

Plant Your Garden

Amid all the talk on a spiritual level about what is soon to occur on planet Earth, the indigenous elders of our planet have a specific piece of practical advice for us all. They have been saying it especially over the last year: it is time to plant your garden. This makes a great deal of sense, whether or not one is spiritual. Just look at what happened in March 2011, with the nuclear reactor disaster in Japan. Many of us realized, with just one event, how endangered our basic food and water sources may be in the event of something catastrophic. The ability to grow one's own food is becoming increasingly important, as our environment grows more toxic and corporate interests seek to control and manipulate our agricultural practices. And there may soon be natural disasters and events that have an effect on worldwide food production, creating food shortages globally.

I have been shown that at some point in the not-too-distant future, our world will look very different from how it looks today. People will, out of necessity and calling, have a much closer relationship to what they eat, to their plants and their water. There will be a movement back to the land and out of cities, and small communities will crop up and grow their own food, becoming almost self-sufficient hamlets, economically speaking. Whether this arises because of a breakdown of the governing and economic systems that rule our lives, or whether this shift happens more peacefully because of the changing consciousness on the planet, the message is the same: it is time to start now, to learn to grow our own food and to take responsibility for our basic sustenance as families and communities.

Many of you have already been doing this. One of the most promising movements of our time, which shows how consciousness is changing, is the permaculture movement. Many people of all walks of life are becoming inspired to live off the grid, to find a sustainable and Earth-honoring way to live, to find solutions based on natural systems. More and more of us are wanting to live more simply, to live closer to the Earth, and to remember the simple beauties and joys in life. Planting a garden is a profound act. You become intimately involved in Mother Earth's miracle of creation. You become tuned in to the reality of birth, growth, and death—and to the reality of what it takes to sustain life. You become a part of something living, mysterious, and divine.

Do we know the plants in our yard? Do we pay attention? By growing gardens, we become intimate with the soil, with the cycles of life, with the food we eat. We start to see that plants also have spirits and respond to love, to positive vibrations and energies. Mother Earth's beautiful plants want to nourish us, to give our bodies exactly what they need to thrive, to heal, and to grow.

There are ways the ancients understood to work with plants and soil that we have forgotten. In the amazing Ringing Cedars series of books from Russia, the extraordinary being Anastasia describes how to imprint soil and seeds with your DNA so that the plant grows in such a way that it gives you exactly what you need for your body. Simply by walking on the soil with bare feet, and by taking seeds in your mouth before planting, you let the plant absorb cellular information about you through your sweat and saliva. The plant then grows encoded with this and can tailor itself to you. These techniques correspond to information I have received, as well. It is important to relate with feeling and love to our plants, especially those that will nourish us. Plants have spirits and want to nourish us. They respond to our emotion, whether it is negative or positive. We can be mindful of creating a harmonious, loving vibration and of interacting with plants as the living spirits they are. It is time to start deepening the way we garden and bringing a higher consciousness to how we think about plants and the living world.

Plants love us and want to help us and feed us, just as Mother Earth herself loves us. The whole of creation is flowing with love. We need to have a relationship with our plants again, to become tender gardeners able to work with Mother Nature to take care of ourselves. This will change our lives and our societies from the ground up. We can start locally and work together on community gardens, or we can grow family gardens—the important thing is to remember what we have forgotten and to do it now. We must plant our gardens, and get our hands dirty, for the sake of a new world.

Gather Your Community

Indigenous elders and wisdom keepers all over the planet are also talking about how, in the future, we will not be so narrowly individualistic. Our survival will depend on our connections with community, and we will work together to get our needs fulfilled and to make sure everyone is cared for. It is said that the time of the lone wolf is over. We are on the verge of a massive shift of consciousness that will change how we relate to each other and how we feel inside.

This may seem like a difficult transition for many of us. After all, haven't we been raised to be individuals and to see ourselves as fundamentally isolated from others? This is a way of life for most of us in the modern world. We are raised not to depend too much on others, to be self-sufficient. Many of us live far away from our families and rely almost exclusively on our spouses or partners for everything. What I have been shown is that this will change drastically in the future. Changes will occur in our societies and in the world as a whole that will bring us together in a new way. We will be brought together. It may not be all pleasant things that will bring us together, but through our shared challenges and even tragedies, we will rediscover our shared humanity. We will once again reach out to each other and will need each other. It may seem unbelievable at this moment, but we will come together as one heart, as the fingers of one hand, and will know that love is why we are here.

It is especially important now to gather with those of like heart and mind and to start developing community. Within a community, there can be sharing of knowledge, skills, resources, inspiration, guidance, and love. Over the last century, human beings in the modern world have overwhelmingly lost this sense of community and connection to a larger human family. We need to reach out and form connections now, to gather with others who share similar dreams and visions for the future, to start co-creating the world we want to see. When things get rough, and in the face of changes likely to come in the next few years, we will need each other, and our survival will depend more on our human connections than on our own wealth, resources, and security. These things may turn out to be an illusion, and we will wonder at how we spent so much of our lives simply in accumulating wealth and security.

Some people are starting communities and trying to create alternate economic models through which many families can live sustainably and in harmony with nature. This is an excellent time to start such a thing or to get involved in its creation. Many people are arranging to leave their urban, high-tech lives to buy a piece of land in the country, where they can live off the grid. Some are even leaving their jobs, inspired by the deeper call of the Earth to live in a whole new way. Though there is no one way that is right for everyone, follow your heart and soul at this time. Trust the guidance your higher self is giving you. If your higher self is calling you to make such a radical change, to start a community or live in one, then listen. You are the co-creator of your life. Your higher self knows what it is you really need to grow and become who you are meant to become.

Even if you cannot live in a community or leave your city life, you can still start to develop your community wherever you are. You can start to reach out, network, share ideas, and form a spiritual group wherever you live. One of the best ways in which to gather together is to start a meditation or sacred action group where you live. It can be devoted to loving and healing Mother Earth or to whatever task you feel called to perform. Gathering together to pray, meditate, or do sacred rituals is a powerful way to create a community of one heart. These communities of the heart are the truest resource when disaster strikes or when the outer world becomes uncertain or unstable. They are our connection with other human beings, with the ability to love and share that will be the gold of the future. As we begin to love Mother Earth, we will naturally love each other more and love ourselves more, too. We will feel compassion and tenderness for all life, ourselves included, and will give that love to others freely. This is what will create a heaven on Earth.

As the Hopi elders have counseled, when in a rapidly flowing river, do not cling to the shore. Do not be afraid to push off into the middle and see who is there with you. We can have a child's trust in the future and face what will come with curiosity, joy, and celebration.

Know that we will be together always. And just as Mother Earth will be reborn into her high heavenly self, we are being reborn, too. We are Spirit and sparks of the divine Love that created us. Never will we not be. We are much greater than we can imagine. Soon we will leave the darkness of the cocoon that was our only world and emerge to find that we have grown wings, and then we will soar. The world will be alive with colors we have never seen; it will be a new world, a new being. The darkness of that long birth will seem like a dream, for finally, we will remember *who we are*.

About Little Grandmother

Kiesha Crowther, "Little Grandmother," began receiving direct teachings from the spirit world and Mother Earth as a child who spent much time alone in the wilderness. She was recognized and initiated as shaman at age thirty and has since been travelling the world doing healing ceremonies for Mother Earth and sharing the messages and teachings she has been given for the benefit of humanity. Her talks, freely available on the web on YouTube and Vimeo, have been viewed by millions of people all over the world. Little Grandmother frequently travels, giving talks and workshops. She lives in Santa Fe, New Mexico. www.littlegrandmother.net

About the Editor

Jennifer Ferraro is a poet, writer, and artist whose work is devoted to illuminating beauty, the soul, and the sacred feminine. She has performed poetry with sacred dance and music and given workshops and presentations for over fifteen years. She has a master of fine arts degree in creative writing and has taught writing at several universities and colleges. She is the author of a book of illustrated poems titled *Divine Nostalgia* and a translation of the ancient mystical poetry of Turkey as well as a forthcoming book about Beauty. She met Kiesha Crowther in 2006.

CPSIA information can be obtained
at www.ICGtesting.com
Printed in the USA
BVHW080642191121
621952BV00004B/244

9 780983 696407